The Very Best Baby Name Book

Edited by
Vera F. Leider

Promotional Sales Books, Inc.
New York, NY

To Emily,
which means industrious,
but more importantly,
it means pure joy and love.

Printed in the United States of America

ISBN: 1-885286-19-8

Contents

Introduction

What's in a name? A very old quotation, but one that is rich with meaning. As you browse through the following pages, you will be amazed at the enormous number of different names from all over the world. For those of you looking for a name for your child, without any preconceived ideas or requirements of what you want, take your time, wander through the words and their definitions.

If, instead, you are looking for a particular ethnic name, for example, we have given you a large variety to choose from. Each name is followed by its ethnic roots, and you will find names from dozens of countries and cultures throughout the world. On the other hand, if you wish to name your child after a loved relative, living or deceased, it is easy to turn directly to the letter you want to use, and try to find a name that is similar and suitable.

Every culture has its own method for choosing names. Some choose the name based on the order of birth. Other babies are named for the day of the week the baby is born, or the name begins with the letter of the day on which the baby is born. Certain Asian customs dictate that parents choose a name that expresses an aesthetic quality or moral characteristic.

There are old names, classic names, and many new names—names that have recently entered our daily lives. Many of these names, as you will see, have been adapted from the classic or traditional names. Many of them are combinations of other names.

Of course, we have not been able, in this short space, to provide every possible name. Instead, the editors tried to compile those names that their research indicated were most popular. Names that were used from Africa were identified by the continent, although some of them may be from specific countries as diverse as Ghana, Kenya,

Uganda, and Zimbabwe. Some names were included to demonstrate their similarities to others from different countries. For example, *Yoki* is an American Indian name that means "rain," or "bluebird on the mesa," while the Japanese name, *Yoko*, means "the positive." Different names and meanings, but very close in spelling.

You will also be fascinated by the hundreds of different names with similar meanings. For example, the following names all mean "*beautiful*."

Alaina (Irish)
Alina (Slavic)
Belle (French)
Bonnie, Bonny (Scottish/ English)
Calla (Greek)
Cho (Korean)
Eu-meh (Chinese)
Farrah (Middle English)
Ghadah (Arabic)
Hasna (Arabic)
Hermosa (Spanish)
Ilona (Hungarian)
Jaffa (Hebrew)
Jamila (Muslim)
Keely (Irish Gaelic)
Mei (Chinese)
Naavah (Hebrew)
Nani (Hawaiian)
Olathe (American Indian)
Shaina (Hebrew)
Vashti (Persian)
Wyanet (American Indian)

In this short list above, there are more than twenty different ways to name your child *beautiful*. Throughout this book you will find many types of names in different languages with similar meanings: God, king, ruler, peace, love, and so on.

Furthermore, many of the names were chosen by our editors entirely on the basis of their having unusual meanings, or meanings that were extremely colorful or interesting, such as many of the American Indian names.

Regardless of how you make your selection, we have found that most people have favorite names that they carry with them into adulthood. These names may be those of former favorite teachers, entertainment figures, friends, relatives, or even their own name. At the same time, we also have memories that were unpleasant, and a name suggested by your mate or friend may evoke that negative memory.

To make your job of choosing a name a little easier, we have provided "worksheets" at the end of the book for Moms and Dads. There is a worksheet for your "Top 10" names; one for boys and one for girls, as well as one for each of parent. Fill in your favorite names from this book, and then rank them in order of preference. Then compare them with your mate's list, and if you're lucky, you'll agree on at least one name (after all, it's *probably* all you'll need). And if not, start with *A* and continue to *Z* for some more names that feel right—this is the first of many decisions ahead—and one of the most fun!

We hope you enjoy perusing through *The Very Best Baby Name Book*, and congratulations on your forthcoming baby!

Girls' Names

A

Aanor (French) variation of Eleanor.

Abbey, Abby common forms of Abigail.

Abbo (African) vegetable

Abelia (French) female form of Abel. *Abella*

Abigail (Hebrew) father of joy. *Abagail, Abbe, Abbey, Abbie, Abby, Gail, Gale*

Abra (Hebrew) earth mother. Female form of Abraham.

Ada (Old English) prosperous; happy. Short form of Adelaide. *Addie, Addy, Adi, Aida*

Adalia (German/Spanish) noble one. *Adal, Adala, Adali, Adalie*

Adara (Greek) beauty; (Arabic) virgin.

Adelaide (Old German) noble; kind. *Addie, Addy, Adela, Adele, Aline, Del, Della*

Adeline English form of Adelaide. *Adaline, Adelina, Adelind, Adella*

Adena (Hebrew) sensuous, voluptuous. *Adina, Dena*

Adina (German) noble, kind.

Adora (Latin) beloved. *Adorée, Dora, Dori, Dorie, Dory*

Adrienne (Latin) dark; rich. *Adrea, Adrianna, Adriena, Hadria*

Afiya (African) health.

Africa (Celtic) pleasant. *Afrika, Africah, Afrikah, Affrica*

Afton (Old English) from Afton.

Agatha (Greek) good; kind. *Ag, Agata, Aggi, Aggie, Aggy*

Agnes (Greek) pure. *Aggie, Agneta, Annis, Ina, Ines, Inez, Nessie, Una, Ynez*

Aida (Italian) form of Ada.

Aileen (Irish) light bearer. Form of Helen. *Aila, Ailee, Ailey, Aili, Alene, Eileen, Elene, Lena*

Aimée (French) form of Amy.

Ainsley (Scottish) from one's own meadow. *Ainslee, Ainslie, Ansley*

Aisha (African) life. *Asha, Ashia, Asia*

Aja (Hindu) goat.

Alaina (Irish) fair, beautiful.

Alameda (Spanish) poplar tree.

Alani (Hawaiian) orange tree.

Alanna (Irish) fair, beautiful. Female form of Alan. *Alana, Alanah, Allene, Lanna*

Alaula (Hawaiian) light of early dawn.

Alberta (Old English) noble, brilliant. Female form of Albert. *Albertina, Alli, Allie, Bert, Berta, Elbertina*

Alcina (Greek) strongminded. *Alcine, Alcinia*

Alea (Arabic) high, exalted. *Aleah*

Aleesha (German) noble; (Greek) truthful. *Aleisha, Alesha, Aleshia, Alesia*

Alethea (Greek) truth. *Alathia, Aletha, Alethia, Alithea, Alithia*

Alexandra (Greek) helper; defender of mankind. Female form of Alexander. *Alessandra, Alexa, Alexia, Alexine, Alexis, Ali, Lexine, Lexy, Sandi, Sandie*

Alfreda (Old English) wise; diplomatic counselor. Female form of Alfred. *Alfi, Elva, Freda, Frieda*

Ali short form of Alexandra. *Alice, Alison.*

Alice (Greek) truth; (German) noble. *Adelaide, Ali, Alika, Alisa, Alisha, Alison, Alissa, Elissa*

Allela, Alisha (English) forms of Alice.

Alida (Greek) beautifully dressed. *Aleda, Leda, Lida*

Alina (Slavic) bright, beautiful. *Aleen, Alena, Alene, Allene*

Aliya (Hebrew) to ascend.

Allegra (Latin) very cheerful. *Allie, Legra*

Allison (Irish) little; truthful; (Old German) famous among the gods. *Ali, Alisha, Alyssa, Lissy*

Alma (Arabic) learned; (Latin) soul.

Almeda (Latin) pressing toward the goal. *Almeta*

Almira (Arabic) exalted. Female form of Elmer. *Almire, Elmira*

Alta (Latin) high.

Althea (Greek) wholesome, healing. *Thea*

Alma (Arabic) learned.

Alva (Spanish/Latin) white; fair.

Alvina (Old English) noble friend. Female form of Alvin. *Alvinia, Vinny*

Alyana (American Indian) eternal bloom.

Alyssa (Greek) logical; sane; alyssum (yellow flower). *Alissa, Allissa, Alysa, Lyssa*

Ama (African) born on Saturday.

Amabel (Latin) lovable. *Amabelle, Belle*

Amanda (Latin) worthy of love. *Manda, Mandi, Mandie, Mandy*

Amara (Greek) eternal beauty. *Amargo, Mara*

Amaris (Hebrew) God's promise.

Amber (Old French) amber. *Amberly*

Amelia (Old German) hard-working. Form of Emily. *Emma, Amalia, Amalita, Amelina, Amy*

Amina (Arabic) security.

Amity (Latin) friendship. *Amitie*

Amy (Latin) beloved. *Aimée, Amata, Emily, Esme*

An (Vietnamese) peace, safety. *Anh*

Anastasia (Greek) of the Resurrection; of springtime. *Ana, Stacey, Stacie, Tasia*

Anatola (Greek) from the east.

Andra (Greek) valiant, strong. *Andree, Andria*

Andrea (Latin) womanly. *Andee, Andie, Andreana, Andree, Andriana*

Angela (Greek) angel, messenger. *Angel, Angelica, Angelina, Angie*

Anisha (Hebrew) gracious. *Anika*

Anita (Spanish) common form of Ann. *Anitra*

Ann, Anne (Hebrew) graceful; (English) form of Hannah. *Anette, Anica, Anissa, Anita, Anitra, Anya, Anna, Annabel, Hanna, Hannie, Hanny, Nanette, Nanice, Nettie, Nina*

Annabel Anna + Belle. *Anabel, Annabella, Annabelle*

Annamaria Anna + Maria. *Annamarie, Annemarie, Annmaria*

Annette common form of Ann.

Annissa form of Annelise. *Anissa*

6

Antoinette (Latin) priceless. Female form of Anthony. *Antonetta, Antonia, Netta, Toni, Tonie*

Anya (Hebrew) gracious.

Aolani (Hawaiian) heavenly cloud.

Aphra (Hebrew) female deer. *Afra*

Apio (African) second of twin sisters.

Aponi (American Indian) butterfly

April (Latin) opening. *Averil, Avril*

Ara (Arabic) rainmaker. *Ari, Aria*

Arabella (Latin) beautiful altar. *Ara, Arabele, Bel, Bella, Belle*

Arantzasu (African) of the Virgin Mary.

Ardelle (Latin) warmth, enthusiasm. *Arda, Ardelia, Ardra*

Arden (Old English) eagle, valley. *Ardenia*

Ardith (Hebrew) flowering field. *Ardath, Ardis, Astra, Ardyth, Aridatha,*

Arella (Hebrew) angel messenger. *Arela*

Aretha (Greek) best. *Retha*

Ariadne (Greek) holy one. Daughter of King Midas. *Ariana, Ariane, Arianie, Arianna*

Ariel (Hebrew) lioness of God. *Aeriel, Ariela, Arielle*

Arin (Hebrew) to sing, to shine, to enlighten.

Arlene (Irish) pledge. Female form of Arlen. *Arlen, Arlena, Arlinda, Arly, Lena*

Asha (Hindi) hope; (Arabic) sunset; living.

Ashley (Old English) from the ash tree meadow. *Ashlee, Ashli*

Astrid (Scandinavian) divine strength.

Astera, Asteria
(Greek) star. *Asta, Astra, Astrea*

Atalanta
(Greek) mighty adversary. *Atlanta, Atlante*

Athena
(Greek) wisdom. *Athene*

Aubrey
(Old French) blond ruler; elf ruler. *Aubree, Aubrette, Aubry*

Audrey
(Old English) noble strength. *Audie, Audra, Audry*

Augusta
(Latin) majestic. Female form of August. *Augustina, Austina, Gussie, Gusta, Tina*

Aurelia
(Latin) golden. *Auria, Aurora, Oralee, Orelia*

Aurora
(Latin) dawn. *Aurelia, Ora, Rora, Rori, Rorie, Rory*

Autumn
(Latin) autumn.

Ava
(Latin) birdlike.

Avery
(Old French) to confirm. *Averi*

Aviva
(Hebrew) springtime. *Avivah, Viva*

Awinita
(American Indian) young deer, fawn.

Ayamé
(Japanese) iris flower

Ayanna
(Hindi) innocent being.

Ayita
(American Indian) the worker; first in the dance.

Ayla
(Hebrew) oak tree.

Azami
(Japanese) thistle flower.

Azar
(Persian) red.

Aziza
(Swahili) precious.

𝓑

Baba (African) born on Thursday

Badria (Afghanistan) moonlike.

Bagamba (African) let them talk.

Bailey (English) fortification.

Barbara (Latin) stranger. *Babette, Babs, Barb, Barbi, Barbra, Bobbie, Bonnie, Bonny*

Barbie common form of Barbara.

Bahira (Arabic) dazzling, brilliant.

Barika (African) bloom; be successful.

Barrie female form of Barry.

Bashiyra (Arabic) joy.

Bathsheba (Hebrew) daughter of Sheba. *Batsheva, Sheba*

Batya (Hebrew) God's daughter. *Bitya*

Bayo (African) found joy.

Beatrice (Latin) bringer of joy. *Bea, Beatrise, Bebe, Bee, Trix, Trixy*

Becky common form of Rebecca.

Belicia (Spanish) dedicated to God. *Bel*

Belle (French) beautiful. *Belinda, Bell, Bella, Belilna, Belva, Belvia, Bill, Billi, Billie, Billy*

Bena (American Indian) pheasant.

Benita (Latin) blessed. Female form of Benedict. *Bendite, Benedetta, Benedicta, Benetta, Benni, Benny, Benoite, Binnie, Binny*

Bernadine (French) brave as a bear. Female form of Bernard. *Berna, Bernadette, Bernadina, Bernita*

Bernice (Greek) bringer of victory. *Bernie, Bunnie, Veronica*

Bertha (Old German) shining. *Berta, Bertina, Birdie*

Beryl (Greek) beryl (seagreen jewel); (Hebrew) precious stone. *Berri, Berrie, Berry, Beryle*

Bessie common form of Elizabeth. *Bess*

Beth (Hebrew) house of God. *Elizabeth*

Bethany (Aramaic) house of poverty.

Betsy, Bette, Betty common forms of Elizabeth.

Beulah (Hebrew) married; a name for Israel.

Beverly (Old English) from the beaver-meadow. *Bev, Beverlee, Bevvy, Buffy, Verlie*

Bianca (Italian) white. Form of Blanche. *Biancha*

Billie (Old English) strong-willed. Common form of Wilhelmina. *Belle, Billi, Billy*

Bina (African) to dance; (Hebrew) wisdom, understanding. *Binah, Buna*

Blaine (Irish) thin, lean. *Blane, Blayne*

Blair (Scottish) plains dweller. *Blaire*

Blake (Old English) one with a swarthy complexion. *Blakelee, Blakeley*

Blanche (Old French) white; fair. *Bellanca, Bianca, Blanca, Blinnie*

Bliss (Old English) bliss, joy. *Blisse*

Blondelle (French) little fair one. *Blondell, Blondie, Blondy*

Blossom (Old English) flowerlike.

Bly (American Indian) high, tall.

Blythe (Old English) joyous. *Blithe*

Bobbi, Bobbie, Bobby common forms of Roberta.

Bong (Korean) Phoenix (mythological bird).

Bonita (Spanish) pretty.

Bonnie, Bonny (Scottish/English) beautiful, pretty. *Bonnee, Bonni*

Brandy (Dutch) brandy (after-dinner drink). *Brandea, Brandi, Brandice, Bree*

Breana (Irish) strong. *Breann, Breanna*

Brenda (Old English) firebrand. Female form of Brandon. *Brendan, Bren, Brenn*

Brenna (Irish) raven; raven-haired. Female form of Brendan. *Bren, Brenn*

Brett (Irish) from Britain. *Brittany.*

Briana (Irish) strong. Female form of Brian. *Breanne, Bria, Brina, Brinna*

Bridget (Irish) resolute strength. *Biddie, Birgitta, Brietta, Brigitte, Brita*

Brina (Slavic) protector. Female form of Brian. *Bryna, Brynna*

Brittany (Latin) from England. *Brett, Brit, Britta, Brittan*

Brooke (Old English) from the brook. Female form of Brook. *Brook, Brooks*

Bunny (English) little rabbit. *Bernice, Bunnie*

Buthaynah (Arabic) with a beautiful, tender body.

C

Caitlin (Irish) form of Catherine. *Catlee, Catlin, Kaitlin, Kaitlyn*

Cala (Arabic) castle.

Calandra (Greek) lark. *Cal, Calandria, Callie, Cally*

Calida (Spanish) warm, ardent. *Callida*

Calla (Greek) beautiful. Short form of Callista. *Cal, Calli, Callie, Cally*

Callista (Greek) most beautiful. *Calista, Calla, Callie, Cally*

Camille (Latin) young ceremonial attendant. *Cam, Camila, Cammi, Milli*

Candace, Candice (Greek) glittering; flowing white. *Candida, Candi, Candie, Candis, Candy, Kandace, Kandy*

Candida (Latin) pure white. *Candace, Candi, Candide, Candie, Candy*

Cantara (Arabic) small bridge.

Caprice (Italian) fanciful.

Cara (Irish) friend; (Latin) dear. *Caralie, Carina, Kara*

Caresse (French) beloved.

Cari (Turkish) flows like water.

Carilla female form of Charles. *Cari, Kari, Karilla*

Carina (Latin) keel. *Carena, Carin, Caryn, Karen, Karena*

Carissa (Greek) loving. *Caresa, Charissa, Karisa*

Carita (Latin) charity. *Caritta, Charity, Karita*

12

Carla short form of Caroline. Female form of Carl or Charles. *Karla*

Carlie, Carly common forms of Caroline; Charlotte. *Carlee, Karlee, Karlie, Karly*

Carlotta (Italian) form of Charlotte.

Carmel (Hebrew) garden. *Carmelina, Carmelita, Lita*

Carmen (Latin) song; (Spanish) from Mount Carmel. *Carma, Carmelina, Carmelita, Carmina, Carmine, Carmita, Charmaine, Karmen*

Carol (Latin) strong; womanly; (French) song of joy. Female form of Carl; Charles. *Carey, Cari, Carleen, Carley, Carlita, Carlota, Carly, Carlyn, Caro, Carola, Carole, Carolina, Caroline, Carolyn, Carolynne, Carrie, Carroll, Carry, Cary, Caryl, Charleen, Charlena, Charlene,*

Charlotta, Charmain, Charmion, Cheryl, Cherlyn, Kari, Karla, Karleen, Karlen, Karole, Karolina, Karyl, Lola, Loleta, Lolita, Lotta, Lotte, Lotti, Lottie, Sharline, Sharyl, Sherrie, Sherry, Sheryl

Caroline, Carolyn (Latin) little and womanly. Modern forms of Carol. Female form of Carl; Charles. *Caria, Carlene, Carley, Carlina, Carline, Carlita, Carlotta, Carlyn, Carol, Carole, Carolin, Carrie, Carroll, Cary, Charlena, Charlene, Karla, Karleen, Karolina, Karolyn*

Casey (Irish) brave. *Casi, Casie, Kacey, Kacie, Kacy, Kasey, Kaycee*

Cassandra (Greek) helper of men. *Casandra, Cass, Cassandre, Cassandry, Cassaundra, Cassi, Cassie, Cassondra, Cassy, Kassandra, Sandi, Sandie, Sandy, Saundra, Sondra,*

Catherine (Greek) pure; (English) form of Katherine. *Caitlin, Cass, Cassie, Catarina, Cate, Cathee, Catherin, Catherina, Cathi, Cathie, Cathlene, Cathrine, Cathryn, Cathy, Catie, Catina, Catrina, Caty*

Cecilia (Latin) blind. Female form of Cecil. *Cecil, Cecile, Cecily, Celia, Celie, Cicely, Cicily, Ciel, Cilka, Cissie, Sisely, Sissy*

Celeste (Latin) heavenly. *Celestina, Celestine, Celia, Celie, Celina, Celisse, Celka, Selestina*

Celia short form of Cecilia.

Chan (Cambodian) sweet-smelling tree.

Chana (Hebrew) grace. *Hannah*

Chandra (Sanskrit) like the moon. *Shandra*

Chantal (French) form of the Latin *cantus* (a song). *Chandal, Chantalle*

Chantrea (Cambodian) moonshine, moon.

Charity (Latin) charity, brotherly love. *Carissa, Carita, Charissa, Charita, Cherri, Cherry*

Charlene common form of Caroline; Charlotte. *Charleen*

Charlotte (French) little and womanly. French form of Carol. Female form of Charles. *Carla, Carleen, Carlene, Carline, Carlota, Carlotta, Carly, Chara, Charil, Charla, Charleen, Charlene, Charline, Charlotta, Charmain, Charmaine, Charmian, Charmion, Charo, Charyl, Cherlyn, Cheryl, Karla, Karleen, Karlene, Karlotta, Karlotte, Lola, Loleta, Lolita, Lotta, Lotte, Lotti, Lottie, Sharleen, Sharlene, Sharline, Sherry, Sherye, Sheryl*

Charmaine (French) common form of Carmen; Charlotte. *Charmain, Charmane, Charmian*

Chastity (Latin) purity.

Chasya (Hebrew) to find shelter.

Chava (Hebrew) life. *Chaya, Eva, Chayka*

Chelsea (Old English) port of ships. *Chelsey, Chelsie, Chelsy*

Cher (French) beloved. *Cherice, Chere, Cherey, Cheri, Cherie, Cherice, Cherise, Cherish, Chery, Cherye, Sher, Sherry, Sherye*

Cherry (Old French) cherry-like. Common form of Charity. *Cherida, Cherri, Cherrita*

Cheryl Common form of Charlotte. *Charyl, Cherianne, Cherilyn, Cherilynn, Shirley*

Chika (Japanese) near. *Chikako*

Chiku (African) chatterer.

Chitsa (American Indian) fair one.

Chloe (Greek) young grass. *Clo, Cloe*

Chloris (Greek) pale; daughter of Niobe. *Cloris*

Cho (Japanese) born at dawn; butterfly; (Korean) beautiful.

Chow (Chinese) summer.

Chris, Chrissy short forms of Christine.

Christabel (Latin/French) beautiful Christian. *Christabella, Cristabel*

Christine (Greek) Christian; anointed. *Cristen, Chris, Chrissie, Chrissy, Christa, Christel, Christen, Christi, Christian, Christiana, Christie, Christin, Christina, Christy, Chrysa, Chrystal, Crista, Cristi, Cristina, Cristine, Cristy, Crystal, Kirsten, Kirstin, Kris, Krissie, Krissy, Kristen, Kristie, Kristin, Kristy, Krysta, Krystyna, Tina*

Chun (Korean) spring.

Cicely (English) form of Cecilia.

Clara (Greek) clear, bright. *Clair, Claire, Clarabelle, Clareta, Clarey, Clarine, Clary, Klarrisa*

Clarissa (Latin/Greek) most brilliant. Modern form of Clara. *Clerissa*

Claudia (Latin) lame. Female form of Claude. *Claudelle, Claudette, Claudie, Claudina*

Clementine (Greek) mercy. *Clem, Clemence, Clementina, Clemmie*

Cleo (Greek) famous. Short form of Cleopatra, the Egyptian queen. *Clea*

Clio (Greek) announcer. Greek muse of history.

Clover (Old English) clover blossom.

Cocheta (American Indian) the unknown.

Cody (Old English) a cushion. *Codee, Codi, Codie*

Colette (Greek/French) victorious in battle. Common form of Nicole. *Collete, Coletta, Collette*

Colleen (Irish) girl. *Colene, Collie, Colline, Colly*

Concepcion (Latin) conception; generation. *Chita, Concha, Conchita*

Concordia (Latin) harmony. Goddess governing peace.

Connie short form of Constance.

Constance (Latin) constancy, firmness. *Conni, Conny, Constantina, Constantine, Costanza*

Consuelo (Spanish) consolation. *Consolata, Consuela*

Cora modern form of Kora. *Corabel, Corabelle, Corena, Corene, Coretta, Corey, Corina, Corinne, Corissa, Corrina*

Cordelia (Welsh) jewel of the sea. *Cordey, Cordie, Cordy, Delia, Della*

Coretta common form of Cora.

Corey (Irish) from the hollow. *Cory, Cori, Kori, Korry*

Corinna, Corinne common forms of Cora. *Coreen, Corine, Corrianne, Corrinne*

Courtney (Old English) from the court. *Cortney, Courtenay, Courtnay, Korney*

Crissy, Cristy short forms of Christine.

Crystal (Latin) clear as crystal. *Christal, Christalle, Christine, Cristal, Crysta, Chrystal, Krystal*

Cybil form of Sibyl.

Cynthia (Greek) moon. *Cinda, Cindee, Cindie, Cindy, Cyndie, Sindee*

D

Dacey (Irish) southerner. *Dacia, Dacie, Dacy, Dasi, Dasie*

Da Chun (Chinese) long spring.

Dada (African) child with curly hair.

Dae (Korean) great.

Dahab (Arabic) gold.

Dahlia (Scandinavian) from the valley. *Dalla*

Daisy (Old English) eye of the day; daisy flower. *Daisey, Daisie*

Dai-tai (Chinese) leading a boy.

Dale (Old English) from the valley. *Dael, Daile, Dayle*

Dalila (African) gentle. *Delilah, Lila*

Dalit (Hebrew) draw water. *Dalis*

Daliyah (Hebrew) a branch. *Daliah*

Dallas (Irish) wise.

Damara (Greek) gentle girl. *Damaris, Mara, Maris*

Damita (Spanish) little noble lady.

Dana (Scandinavian) from Denmark. *Dayna, Tana*

Danae (Greek). Mythological mother of Perseus. *Dee, Denae, Dene*

Danica (Slavic) morning star. *Danika*

Danielle (Hebrew) judged by God. Female form of Daniel. *Danella, Danelle, Daniela, Danna*

Daphne (Greek) laurel tree. *Daffi, Daffie, Daffy, Daphna*

Dara (Hebrew) compassion. *Darya*

Darby (Irish) free man. *Darb, Darbie*

Darcie, Darcy (Irish) dark. *Darcee, Darcey, Darice*

Daria (Greek) queenly. Female form of Darius. *Dari*

Darlene (Old French) little darling. *Dareen, Darla, Darline, Darrelle, Darryl*

Davida (Hebrew) beloved. Female form of David. *Daveta, Davi, Davina, Veda, Vida*

Dawn (Old English) dawn.

Dayo (African) joy arrives.

Deanna common form of Dena; Diana. Female form of Dean. *Deana, Deanna, Deanne*

Deborah (Hebrew) bee. Hebrew prophetess. *Deb, Debbie, Debra, Devora*

Dee (Welsh) black, dark. Short form of Deirdre; Delia; Diana. *Dede, Dee Dee, Deanna, Didi*

Deirdre (Irish) sorrow; complete wanderer. *Dede, Dee, Deidre, Didi*

Delaney (Irish) descendent of the challenger. *Delaney, Delanie*

Delia (Greek) visible; moon goddess; from Delos. Short form of Cordelia. *Adelaide, Dee, Dede, Dehlia, Dela, Delinda*

Delilah (Hebrew) brooding; companion of Samson. *Dalila, Delila, Lilah*

Della common form of Adelaide; Delia.

Delphine (Greek) calmness. *Delfeena, Delfine, Delphina, Delphinia*

Dembe (African) peace.

Dena (Hebrew) vindicated; (Old English/American Indian) from the valley. Female form of Dean. *Deana, Deanna, Deena, Deeyn, Diana, Dina, Dinah*

Denise (French) believer in Dionysus (god of wine). Female form of Dennis. *Deni, Denice, Denny, Dinny*

Derya (Hawaiian) ocean.

Desiree (French) longed. *Desirae, Désiree, Desiri*

Desta (Ethiopian) happiness.

Destinee (Old French) destiny.

Devin (Irish) poet. *Devan, Devinne*

Devonna (Old English) defender (of Devonshire). *Devon, Devondra, Devonne*

Dezba (American Indian) going to war.

Diana (Latin) divine; goddess of the hunt, the moon, and fertility. *Deana, Deanna, Di, Diahann, Diandra, Diane, Dianna, Dyan*

Dinah (Hebrew) vindicated; daughter of Jacob and Leah. *Dena, Diana, Dina, Dyna, Dynah*

Dionne (Greek) divine queen; mother of Aphrodite. *Deonne, Dion, Dionis*

Do (African) first child after twins.

Dodie (Hebrew) beloved. Common form of Dora. *Dodi, Dody*

Dofi (African) next child after twins.

Dolly fommon form of Dorothy. *Dolley, Dollie*

Dolores (Spanish) sorrows. *Delora, Deloria, Deloris, Dolorita, Doloritas, Lola, Lolita*

Dominique
(French/Latin) belonging to God. Female form of Dominic. *Domeniga, Dominga, Domini, Dominica*

Donna
(Latin/Italian) lady. *Dona, Donella, Donetta, Donia, Ladonna*

Donoma
(American Indian) visible sun.

Dora
(Greek) gift. Common form of Dorothy. *Dodi, Doralia, Doralyn, Doreen, Dorelia, Dorella, Dorelle, Dorena, Dorene, Doretta, Dorette, Dorey, Dori, Dorie, Doris, Dorita*

Doreen
(Irish) sullen. Common form of Dora. *Dorene, Dorine*

Dori, Dory
common forms of Dora; Doria; Doris; Dorothy.

Doria
(Greek) female form of Dorian. *Dori, Dorian, Dorice, Doris, Dory, Dorree*

Doris
(Greek) from the sea. *Dori, Doria, Dorice, Dorisa, Dorita, Dorrie, Dory*

Dorothy
(Greek) gift of God. *Dasha, Dode, Dody, Doll, Dolley, Dora, Dorthea, Dory, Dosi, Dot, Dotti*

Dottie, Dotty
common forms of Dorothy.

Dulcie
(Latin) sweetness. *Delcina, Delcine, Dulce, Dulcea, Dulcia, Dulcine, Dulcinea, Dulcy, Dulsea*

Dusty
female form of Dustin.

Dyani
(American Indian) deer.

E

Earla female form of Earl. *Earleen, Earlene, Erlene, Erlina, Erline*

Eartha (Old English) of the earth. *Erda, Ertha, Herta, Hertha*

Ebony (Greek) a hard, dark wood. *Ebonee*

Eden (Hebrew) delight. *Edin*

Edie short form of Edith.

Edith (Old English) rich gift. *Dita, Edie, Edita, Ediva, Edy*

Edna (Hebrew) rejuvenation. *Eddi, Eddie, Eddy*

Edwina (Old English) prosperous friend. Female form of Edwin. *Edina, Edwyna, Win, Wina*

Efia (African) born on Friday.

Eileen (Irish) form of Helen.

Ekika (Hawaiian) rich gift.

Elaine (French) form of Helen. *Elana, Elane, Elayne, Lainey, Layney*

Eldora (Spanish) golden, gilded. Female form of Eldorado. *Eldoree, Eldoria*

Eleanor (Greek) light. Form of Helen. *Eleanora, Eleanore, Elinor, Ella, Elle, Ellen, Elly, Elna, Elora, Lena, Leora, Nell, Nora*

Electra (Greek) shining, brilliant.

Elenola (Hawaiian) light. Form of Eleanor.

Elia (Hebrew) Jehovah is God.

Elise (French) common form of Elizabeth. *Elysia.*

22

Elissa common form of Alice; Elizabeth.

Elizabeth (Hebrew) oath of God. *Belita, Belle, Bess, Bessie, Beth, Betsey, Betsy, Bette, Bettina, Betty, Elisa, Elisabet, Ellsabeth, Elise, Elissa, Eliza, Elizabet, Elsa, Elsbeth, Elsie, Elspeth, Elyse, Isabel, Libbey, Libbi, Libbie, Libby, Lisa, Lisabeth, Lise, Lisette, Lissa, Lissy, Lizabeth, Lizbeth, Lizzie, Ysabel*

Elke common form of Alice; Alexandra. *Elka*

Ella (Old English) elf; beautiful fairy woman. *Ellette, Elli, Ellie, Elly*

Ellen (English) form of Helen. *Ellene, Ellie, Elly, Ellyn*

Elsa (Old German) noble. Common form of Elizabeth. *Else, Elsie, Elsy, Ilsa, Ilse*

Elsie, Elsy forms of Elsa; Elizabeth.

Elvira (Spanish) white; fair. *Elva, Elvera, Elvina, Elvire, Elwira, Lira*

Elysia (Latin) sweetly blissful. *Elicia, Elise, Elisha, Elyse, Elysha*

Emalia (Hawaiian) industrious. Form of Emily.

Eme (Hawaiian) beloved. Form of Amy.

Emily (Old German) industrious; (Latin) flatterer. Form of Amelia; Female form of Emil. *Amalie, Amelia, Amelita, Em, Emalee, Emelita, Emera, Emilee, Emili, Emilia, Emilie, Emiline, Emlynne, Emma, Emmalee, Emmaline, Emmalyn, Emmey, Emmi, Emmie, Emmy*

Emma (Old German) universal; nurse. Short form of Emily. *Amy, Em, Ema, Emelina, Emmaline, Emmi*

Enid (Welsh) purity; woodlark.

Erica (Scandinavian) ever-powerful. Female form of Eric. *Ericha, Ericka, Ricki, Rikki*

Erin (Irish) peace; name for Ireland. *Aryn, Eran, Erinn, Erinna, Eryn*

Esmeralda (Spanish, Greek) emerald. *Esma, Esmaria, Esme, Ezmeralda*

Estelle (Old French) star. *Estele, Estella, Estrella, Estrellita, Stella*

Esther (Persian) star. *Stella, Essa, Essie, Ettie, Hester, Hettie*

Etana (Hebrew) strong. Female form of Ethan.

Ethel (Old English) noble. *Ethelda, Etheline, Ethelyn, Ethyl*

Etsu (Japanese) delight.

Etta (Old German) little. Common form of Henrietta. *Etty*

Eudora (Greek) honored. *Dora*

Eugenia (Greek) well-born. Female form of Eugene. *Eugenie, Gene, Genia*

Eulalia (French/Greek) fair of speech. *Eula, Eulalee, Eulalie*

Eu-meh (Chinese) especially beautiful.

Eunice (Greek) happy victory.

Eva short form of Evangeline; a form of Eve.

Evangeline (Greek) bearer of good tidings. *Eva, Evangelia, Eve*

Evania (Greek) tranquil, untroubled. *Evanne*

Eve (Hebrew) life; wife of Adam. *Eba, Ebba, Eva, Evelina, Evelyn, Evey, Evita, Evonne*

Evetta (African) hunt. *Evette*

F

Fabayo (African) lucky birth is joyful.

Fadilah (Arabic) virtue.

Faith (Middle English) fidelity. *Fae, Fay, Faye, Fayth, Faythe*

Fala (American Indian) crow.

Falak (Arabic) star.

Faline (Latin) catlike.

Fallon (Irish) grandchild of the ruler.

Fanny common form of Frances. *Fan, Fannie*

Far (Chinese) flower.

Faraji (African) consolation.

Farrah (Middle English) beautiful; pleasant. *Fara, Farah, Farand, Farra*

Fatima (Arabic) unknown; daughter of Muhammad, the Prophet. *Fatimah, Fatma*

Fatuma (African) weaned.

Fawn (Old French) young deer. *Faina, Faun, Faunia*

Fay (Old French) fairy; elf. *Fae, Faith, Faye, Fayette, Fayina*

Fayola (African) good fortune walks with honor.

Felicia (Latin) happy. Female form of Felix. *Felice, Felicidad, Felicity, Felise, Felisha, Felita*

Fern (Old English) fern. Short form of Fernanda. *Ferne*

Femi (African) love me.

Fernanda (Old German) adventurer. Female form of Ferdinand. *Fem, Femande, Fernandina*

Fidelity (Latin) faithfulness. *Faith, Fidela, Fidelia*

Fiona (Irish) fair. *Fionna*

Fionnula (Irish) white-shouldered. *Fenella, Finella*

Flavia (Latin) blonde, yellow-haired.

Flo (American Indian) like an arrow.

Flora (Latin) flower. Short form of Florence. *Fiora, Fiore, Fleur, Flo, Flor, Florella, Floria, Floris, Florrie*

Florence (Latin) blooming; prosperous. *Flo, Flora, Florencia, Flori, Florida, Florie, Florinda, Florine*

Florida (Latin) flowery, blooming; (Spanish) form of Florence. *Floridia*

Folayan (African) walk with dignity.

Fowzia (Afghanistan) productive.

Frances (Latin) free; a form of Freda; (French) female form of Francis. *Fan, Fanchette, Fanchon, Fancie, Fania, Fannie, Fanny, Fanya, Fran, Francesca, Franci, Francie, Francine*

Freda (Old German) peaceful. Short form of Frederica. *Frayda, Fredella, Freida*

Frederica (Old German) peaceful ruler. Female form of Frederick. *Farica, Federica, Freddi, Freddie, Fredia, Rica, Ricki*

Freya (Scandinavian) noble woman; the goddess Freya. *Fraya*

Frumit (Hebrew) pious, religious. *Fruma*

Fung (Chinese) bird.

Fuyu (Japanese) born in winter.

G

Gabrielle (Hebrew) strength in God. Female form of Gabriel. *Gabbey, Gabey, Gabie, Gabriela, Gabriella, Gabrila, Gavrielle*

Gaho (American Indian) mother.

Gail (Old English) gay, lively. Short form of Abigail. Form of Gay. *Gael, Gale, Gayla, Gayle, Gayleen, Gaylene*

Galina (Russian) form of Helen.

Galia (Hebrew) God has redeemed. *Galya*

Galilahi (American Indian) amiable; attractive.

Galit (Hebrew) fountain.

Garnet (Middle English) garnet (a dark red gem). *Garnette*

Ganesa (Indian) god of good luck and widsom.

Ganit (Hebrew) garden. *Gana, Ganice*

Garbiñe (Spanish/Basque) purification.

Garuda (Indian/Hindi) sun bird ridden by the god Vishnu.

Gavrila (Hebrew) heroine; strong. Female form of Gabriel. *Gavriella, Gavrielle, Gavrilla*

Gay (Old French) merry. Form of Gail. *Abigail, Gae, Gaye*

Geetha (Indian/Hindi) song, from Hindu lyrics.

Gella (Hebrew) yellow.

Gemini (Greek) twin. *Gemina*

Gemma (Latin/Italian) jewel, precious stone. *Jemma*

Gen (Japanese) source, spring.

Genat (Ethiopian) heaven.

Gene form of Jean.

Geneva (Old French) juniper tree. Short form of Genevieve. *Gena, Genevra, Janeva, Jennifer*

Genevieve (Old German/French) white wave. Form of Guinevere. *Gena, Geneva, Genevieve, Genevra, Gennie, Genny, Genovera, Gina, Jennie, Jennifer, Jenny*

Georgeanne common form of Georgia. *Georgeanna, Georgetta, Georgiana, Georgianna, Georgianne*

Georgia (Latin) farmer. Female form of George. *Georgeanna, Georgena, Georgeta, Georgette, Georgianne, Georgina*

Geraldine (Old German/French) mighty with the spear. Female form of Gerald. *Deena, Deena, Geraldina, Gerianne, Gerrie, Gerrilee, Jeralee, Jeri*

Geri, Gerri, Gerrie, Gerry short forms of Geraldine.

Germaine (French) German. *Germain, Germana, Jermaine*

Gertrude (Old German) spear strength; warrior woman. *Gerda, Gert, Gerta, Gerti, Gertrud, Gertruda, Gertrudis, Gerty, Trude, Trudi, Trudie, Trudy*

Ghadah (Arabic) beautiful.

Ghaliyah (Arabic) fragrant.

Gi (Korean) brave; foundation.

Gigi common form of Gilberte; Giselle.

Gilberte (Old German) brilliant pledge. Female form of Gilbert. *Berta, Berte, Berti, Gigi, Gilberta, Gilbertina, Gill, Gilli*

Gilda (Old English) covered with gold. *Golda*

Gilit (Hebrew) joy. *Gilia, Gili, Gilal*

Gin (Japanese) silver. *Gina*

Gina common form of Angelina; Regina. *Jena*

Ginger (Latin) ginger (flower or spice). Common form of Virginia.

Ginny common form of Virginia.

Giselle (Old German) pledge; hostage. *Gisela, Gisele*

Gladys (Celtic) princess; (Latin) small sword; gladiolus flower; (Welsh) form of Claudia. *Glad, Gladi, Gleda*

Glenda form of Glenna.

Glenna (Irish) from the valley or glen. Female form of Glenn. *Glenda, Glenine, Glenn, Glennie, Glennis, Glyn, Glynis, Glynnis*

Gloria (Latin) glory. *Glori, Gloriana, Gloriane, Glory*

Glynis (Welsh) form of Glenna. *Glynnis*

Golda (Old English) gold. *Gilda, Goldi, Goldia, Goldina, Goldy*

Golna (Persian) center of flame; red flower.

Goo (Korean) completeness.

Grace (Latin) graceful. *Engracia, Gracia, Gracie, Grata, Gratia, Gratiana, Grayce, Grazia*

Grazyna (Slavic) grace.

Greer (Scottish) short female form of Gregor (from Gregory). *Grier*

Gregoria (Greek) watchful.

Greta (German) short form of Margaret. *Gretchen, Grete, Gretel, Gretna, Gretta*

Gretchen (German) form of Margaret.

Griselda (Old German) gray woman warrior. *Grishilda, Grissel, Grizelda, Selda, Zelda*

Guan-yin (Chinese) goddess of mercy.

Guinevere (Welsh) white, fair; white wave; wife of King Arthur. *Freddi, Gaynor, Genevieve, Genna, Gennifer, Genny, Ginevra, Gwendolyn, Guenevere, Guenna, Guinna, Gwen, Gwenora, Gwenore, Janifer, Jen, Jenni, Jennie, Jennifer, Jenny, Oona, Una, Winni, Winnie, Winny*

Gulalai (Afghanistan) flower.

Guri (Indian/Hindu) goddess of abundance.

Gustha (Teutonic) staff of the gods. Form of Gustava.

Guta (Hebrew) good.

Gwen short form of Guinevere; Gwendolyn.

Gwendolyn (Welsh) white; white-browed. *Guenna, Gwen, Gwendolen, Gwendolin, Gwenette, Gwenni, Gwennie, Gwenny, Gwyn, Gwyneth, Gwynne, Wanda, Wendi, Wendie, Wendy, Wynne*

Gwyneth (Welsh) white; blessed. Form of Gwendolyn. *Gwynne, Winnie, Winny, Wynne, Wynnie, Wynny*

H

Habibah (Arabic) beloved.

Hadar (Hebrew) ornament.

Hadara (Hebrew) splendor.

Hadiya (African) gift. *Hadiyah*

Hagar (Hebrew) flight.

Haley (Scandinavian) hero. *Hailee, Haily, Haleigh, Halie, Hally, Hayley*

Halla (African) unexpected gift.

Hallie (Greek) thinking of the sea. *Halette, Hali, Halimeda, Halley, Halli, Hally*

Haloke (American Indian) salmon.

Halona (American Indian) fortunate.

Hamidah (Arabic) praiseworthy.

Hana (Japanese) flower; (German) form of Hannah. *Hanae, Hanako*

Hanako (Japanese) flower. *Hana, Hanae*

Hannah (Hebrew) graceful; mother of Samuel. Form of Ann. *Hana, Hanna, Hanni, Hannie, Hanny, Honna*

Harley (Old English) from the long field. *Harlene, Harli, Harlie*

Harmony (Latin) harmony. *Harmonia, Harmonie*

Harriet (Old French) ruler of the home. Female form of Harry. *Harri, Harrie, Harrietta, Harriette, Harriot, Hatti, Henrietta*

Haruko (Japanese) tranquil, spring-born.

31

Hasanti (African) good.

Hasna (Arabic) beautiful.

Hateya (American Indian) press with the foot.

Haunani (Hawaiian) beautiful dew.

Hazel (Old English) hazelnut tree; commanding authority. *Aveline*

Healoha (Hawaiian) loved one.

Heather (Middle English) flowering heather. *Heath*

Hee (Korean) pleasure.

Hedda (Old German) strife. *Heda, Hedi, Heddi, Heddie, Hedwig, Hedwiga*

Hei (Korean) grace; wisdom. *Hye*

Heidi short form of the German name Adalheid. *Heida, Heidie*

Helen (Greek) light. *Aila, Aileen, Ailene, Eileen, Elaine, Elana, Elane, Elayne, Eleanor, Eleanore, Elena, Elene, Elinora, Elinor, Ella, Elladine, Elle, Ellen, Elli, Ellie, Elna, Elnora, Elyn, Helaina, Helena, Helene, Helenka, Helli, Jelena, Lana, Leanor, Leena, Lena, Lenora, Leonore, Leora, Lina, Lora, Nell, Nellie, Nelly, Nora, Norah*

Helga (Old German) pious. Form of Olga.

Heloise (French) form of Eloise.

Henrietta (French) mistress of the household. Female form of Henry. *Enriqueta, Etta, Ettie, Hattie, Hatty, Henka, Henrie, Henrieta, Henriette, Hetty, Yetta, Yettie*

Hermione (Greek) of the earth. *Erma, Hermia, Hermina, Hermine, Herminia, Irma*

Hermosa (Spanish) beautiful.

Hester (Greek) star; (Dutch) form of Esther. *Hestia, Hettie, Hetty*

Hestia (Persion) a star. Goddess of the home.

Hidéyo (Japanese) superior generations.

Hilary (Greek) cheerful; merry. *Hillary, Hilliary*

Hilda (Old German) woman warrior. Short form of Hildegarde. *Hilde, Hildy*

Hildegarde (Old German) fortress. *Hilda, Hildagard, Hildagarde*

Hinda (Hebrew) hind female deer. *Hynda*

Hisa (Japanese) long-lasting. *Hisako, Hisae, Hisayo*

Hokulani (Hawaiian) star in the heaven.

Holly (Old English) holly tree. *Holli, Hollie*

Honey (Old English) sweet.

Honora (Latin) honorable. *Honey, Honor, Honoria, Honorine, Nora, Norah, Norri, Norrie, Norry*

Honovi (American Indian) strong deer.

Hope (Old English) hope.

Hoshi (Japanese) star.

Howin (Chinese) loyal swallow.

Hula (Chinese) flower.

Hulda (Hebrew) weasel.

Huyana (American Indian) falling rain.

Hyacinth (Greek) hyacinth flower. *Hyacinthia, Jacinda, Jacinta*

Hyo (Korean) filial duty.

Hyun (Korean) wisdom.

I

Ibtihaj (Arabic) joy.

Ida (Old English) prosperous; (Old German) hard-working. *Idalia, Idalina, Idaline, Idell*

Ifama (African) everything is fine.

Ignacia (Latin) ardent fiery. Female form of Ignatius. *Ignatia*

Ihilani (Hawaiian) heavenly splendor.

Iku (Japanese) nourishing.

Ikuseghan (African) peace surpasses war.

Ilana (Hebrew) tree, big tree. *Ilanit*

Ilene form of Aileen.

Ilima (Hawaiian) name of a yellow flower.

Ilona (Hungarian) beautiful. Form of Helen. *Ilonka*

Ilsa form of Elsa.

Imala (American Indian) disciplinarian.

Iman (Arabic) faith; belief.

Imena (African) a dream.

Imogene (Latin) image. *Emogene, Imogen, Imojean*

Ina (Latin) female suffix added to masculine names; (Irish) form of Agnes. *Ina, Inga*

Inez (Spanish) form of Agnes. *Ines, Inesita, Ynes, Ynez*

Inda (Hebrew) pleasure. *Inde*

Inga, Inge (Scandinavian) old Germanic hero. Form of Ingrid.

Ingrid (Scandinavian) hero's daughter. *Inga, Inge, Inger*

Iola (Greek) dawn cloud; violet-colored. *Iole*

Ione (Greek) violet-colored stone. *Iona*

Iphigenia (Greek) sacrifice. Daughter of the Greek leader Agamemnon. *Genia*

Irene (Greek) peace. Goddess of peace. *Ira, Irena, Irina, Rena, Rina*

Iris (Greek) rainbow. Goddess of the rainbow and messenger of the gods. *Irisa, Irita*

Irma (Latin) noble. *Erma, Hermione, Irmina*

Isabel (Old Spanish) consecrated to God; (Spanish) form of Elizabeth. *Belicia, Belita, Belle, Isabella, Izabel*

Isadora (Latin) gift of Isis. Female form of Isador. *Isidora*

Isamu (Japanese) vigorous, robust.

Isolde (Welsh) fair lady. Princess in the Arthurian legends. *Isolda*

Istas (American Indian) snow.

Ito (Japanese) thread.

Iverem (African) blessing and favor.

Ivory (Latin) made of Ivory.

Ivy (Old English) ivy tree. *Ivie*

Iwa (Japanese) rock.

Izegbe (African) long-awaited child.

Izusa (American Indian) white stone.

J

Jacalyn (Hebrew) to supplant.

Jacey Combination of initials J + C.

Jacinda (Greek) beautiful, comely; hyacinth flower. Form of Hyacinth. *Jacenta, Jacey, Jacie, Jacinta, Jacy, Jacynth*

Jackie short form of Jacoba; Jacqueline.

Jacoba (Hebrew) supplanter. Female form of Jacob. *Jacki, Jackie, Jacobina*

Jacqueline (Hebrew) supplanter; (Old French) little Jacques. Female form of Jacob (through Jacques). *Jacklyn, Jaquelin, Jaquith*

Jade (Spanish) jade. *Jada*

Jael (Hebrew) to ascend.

Jaffa (Hebrew) beautiful.

Jaime (French) I love. *Amy, Jaime*

Jaha (African) dignity.

Jala (Arabic) clarity; elucidation.

Jamie female form of James. *Jaimie, Jammie, Jaymee*

Jamila (Muslim) beautiful. *Jamilla, Jamille*

Jane (Hebrew) God is gracious. Female form of John. *Jaine, Jana, Janaye, Janella, Janet, Janice, Janie, Janine, Janis*

Janna (Arabic) a harvest of fruit. Form of Johanna.

Jardena (Hebrew) to flow downward. Female form of Jordan.

Jarietta (Arabic) earthen water jug. *Jarita*

Jasmine (Persian)
jasmine flower. *Jasmina, Jazmin, Jess, Yasmeen*

Jay (Medieval Latin)
jaybird. *Jae, Jaycee, Jaye*

Jean, Jeanne
(Scottish) forms of Jane; Joan. *Jeanette, Jeannie, Jennica, Jennine*

Jemima (Hebrew) dove.
Jamima, Jemimah, Jemie, Jemmie, Jemmy

Jena (Arabic) a small
bird. *Jenna*

Jennifer (Welsh) white
fair. Form of Guinevere. *Genevieve, Gwendolyn, Ginnifer, Jenifer, Jenna, Jennica, Jennilee, Jenny*

Jenny form of Jane;
Jennifer.

Jerrie, Jerry short forms
of Geraldine. *Jeri, Jerrilee, Jerrylee*

Jessica (Hebrew)
wealthy. Female form of Jesse. *Jasmine, Jess, Jessalyn, Jesselyn, Jessie*

Jessie short form of
Jasmine; Jessica. (Scottish) common form of Janet. *Jessa, Jesse, Jessi*

Jewel (Old French)
precious gem. *Jewell, Jewelle*

Jezebel (Hebrew)
unexalted; impure. Wife of King Ahab. *Jessabell, Jezabella, Jezabelle*

Jill common form of
Gillian. *Jillana, Jillane, Jilleen, Jilli*

Jillian (Latin) young
downy-haired child. *Gillian, Jill, Jillana, Jillie, Julia.*

Jin (Korean) jewel; truth.
Gin

Jinny (American)
common form of Virginia; (Scottish) common form of Jenny.

Jo short form of Joan;
Joanna; Josephine.

Joan (Hebrew) God is
gracious. Form of Jane. Female form of John. *Joane, Joanie, Jodi, Joni*

Joanna, Joanne
common forms of Jane. Female forms of John. *Jo, Jo Ann, Jo-Ann, Johanna*

Joby (Hebrew)
persecuted. Female form of Job. *Jobey, Jobina, Jobye, Jobyna*

Jocelyn (Latin) merry;
(Old English) just. *Jocelin, Joceline, Josselyn, Joyce, Justine*

Jodi, Jody common
forms of Joan; Judith. *Jodee, Jodie*

Joelle (Hebrew) the Lord
is willing. Female form of Joel. *Joella, Joellen, Joelly, Joelynn*

Johnna female form of
John; form of Johanna. *Giana, Jonell, Jonis*

Jolene (Middle English)
he will increase. Female form of Joseph. *Joleen, Joline, Jolyn*

Jordan (Hebrew)
descending. *Jordana, Jorey, Jori, Jorry*

Josephine (Hebrew) he
shall increase. Female form of Joseph. *Fifi, Jo, Joette, Joline, Josee, Josefina, Josy*

Joy (Latin) joy. *Joya,
Joyan, Joyann, Joyce*

Joyce (Latin) joyous.
Jocelyn, Jolce, Joy, Joyous

Juanita (Spanish)
common form of Joan. *Juana, Waneta*

Judith (Hebrew) of Judah.
Jody, Juditha, Judy

Judy short form of Judith.
Judi, Judye

Julia (Latin) youthful.
Female form of Julius. *Joletta, Julee, Juliana, Julianne, Juliet, Julleta, Julina, Julissa*

Julie form of Julia. *Juline*

June (Latin) June.
Junette, Junia

Justine (Latin) just.
Female form of Justin. *Justina, Justinn*

K

Kachina (American Indian) sacred dancer.

Kacy (Irish) brave. *Kacey, Kaci, Kacie*

Kady (Greek) pure, unsullied. *Katherine*

Kaela (Arabic) beloved. *Kaelyn, Kaila, Kailee, Kailey*

Kala (Hindi) black; time.

Kali (Sanskrit) energy.

Kalinda (Sanskrit) sun. *Kaleena, Kalina, Kalindi*

Kalola (Hawaiian) song of joy.

Kama (Sanskrit) love. Mythological Hindu god of love.

Kamaria (African) like the moon.

Kameko (Japanese) child of the tortoise.

Kamilah (Arabic) the perfect one. *Kamila, Kamillah*

Kanya (Hindu) virgin. *Kania*

Kara form of Cara; common form of Katherine. *Karalee, Karrah*

Karen (Danish) form of Katherine. *Carin, Caryn, Karin, Karna, Karyn, Kerrin*

Kari common form of Katherine. *Karee, Karie, Karilynn, Karylin*

Karla form of Caroline; Charlotte.

Kate short form of Katherine.

Katherine (Greek) pure. *Caitlin, Caitrin, Cassie, Catarina, Catharine, Cathee, Catlaina, Karena, Katina, Katrina, Katya, Ketti*

Kathleen (Irish) form of Katherine. *Kathlin, Katleen, Katlin*

Kathy short form of Katherine. *Kathleen, Kathryn.*

Katie short form of Katherine. *Katee, Kati, Katy*

Katrina (Greek) form of Katherine. *Catrina, Katine*

Kayla form of Kay; Katherine. *Cayla, Kaela, Kaila, Kaylyn*

Keely (Irish Gaelic) beautiful. *Keeley, Keelia*

Keiko (Japanese) adored.

Kelila, Kelula (Hebrew) crown; laurel. *Kaile, Kayla, Kaylee, Kyla*

Kelly (Irish Gaelic) warrior woman. *Kelley, Kellen, Kelli, Kellia, Kellie, Kellina*

Kelsey (Scandinavian) from the ship island. *Kelci, Kellsie, Kelsy*

Kendra (Old English) knowledgeable. *Kendre, Kinna*

Kerry (Irish Gaelic) dark; dark-haired. *Keri, Kerianne*

Kimberly (Old English) from the royal fortress. *Kim, Kimberlee, Kimbra, Kimmie, Kym*

Kiona (American Indian) brown hills.

Kip, Kipp (Old English) from the pointed hill. *Kippie, Kippy*

Kira (Persian) sun. Female form of Cyrus.

Kirby (Old English) from the church town. *Kirbee, Kirbie*

Kirsten (Scandinavian) form of Christine. *Kiersten, Kirsti, Kirstin, Kristyn*

Koko (American Indian) night.

Kora (Greek) maiden. Daughter of Demeter, goddess of agriculture. *Cora, Corabel, Corena, Corey, Cori, Corie, Corissa, Corrina, Korella, Koren, Korie*

Kristen (Scandinavian) form of Christine. *Krista, Kristel, Kristi, Kristina, Kristyn*

Kristina, Kristine forms of Christina; Christine.

Krystal form of Crystal. *Kristal, Krystle*

Kunto (African) third child.

Kuulei (Hawaiian) my child.

Kyle (Irish Gaelic) handsome; living near the chapel. *Kiley, Kyla, Kylie, Kylynn*

41

L

Lacey (Latin) cheerful. Common form of Larissa. *Lacee, Laci, Lacie, Lacy*

Ladonna (French) the lady.

Lahela (Hawaiian) innocence of a lamb.

Leilani (Hawaiian) heavenly child.

Lainey (English) common form of Elaine.

Lakisha Combination of La + Aisha. *Lakesha, Lakeshia, Laquisha*

Lana (English) form of Helen. Short form of Alanna. *Lanette, Lanny*

Lane (Middle English) from the narrow road. *Laina, Laney, Lanny, Layne*

Lani (Hawaiian) sky, heaven. *Lanita*

Lara (Latin) shining; famous. *Laraine, Laura, Lorraine*

Laraine (Latin) sea-bird; gull. Form of Lorraine. *Lara, Laura, Larina, Larine*

Larissa (Greek) cheerful. *Lacey, Laryssa, Lissa*

Lark (Middle English) skylark.

Latasha Combination of La + Tasha. *Latashia, Latesha, Latisha, Latosha, Leticia, Letisha, Letitia.*

Lateefah (African) gentle; pleasant.

Latona (Greek) powerful, mythological deity. *Latonia, Latoya, Latoye, Latoyia*

Latrice diminutive form of Letitia. *Latricia, Letreece*

Laura (Latin) crown of laurel leaves. Female form of Lawrence. *Lara, Laraine, Lorraine, Laurel, Lauren, Laurena, Lauretta, Lora, Loren, Loretta, Lorette, Lori, Lorinda, Lorita, Lorna, Lorre, Lorrie, Lorry*

Lauren (English) form of Laura. *Lauryn, Lorre, Lorrin*

Lavelle (Latin) cleansing. *Lavella*

Laverne (Old French) from the grove of alder trees; (Latin) springlike. *Laverna, La Verne, Vema*

Lavinia (Latin) purified. *Lavena, Lavina, Lavinie, Vin, Vinni, Vinnie, Vinny*

Lawanda (Spanish) form of Joanna. Combination of La + Wanda; from Lajuan.

Layla (African) born at night.

Leah (Hebrew) weary; wife of Jacob. *Lea, Lee, Leigh*

Leandra (Latin) like a lioness. *Leodora, Leoline, Leonelle*

Leda (Greek) lady. Common form of Letitia. *Leta, Lida*

Lee (Irish Gaelic) poetic;(Old English) pasture, meadow; (Chinese) plum. Short form of Leah. *Leann, Leanna, Leeann, Leeanne, LeeAnn, Leigh*

Leila (Arabic) dark as night. *Layla, Leilah, Lela, Leland*

Leilani (Hawaiian) heavenly flower. *Lani.*

Lena (Latin) temptress. Short form of names ending in -leen , -lena , -lina, and -line. *Lenee, Lina*

Lenore (Russian) form of Eleanor. *Lenora, Leonor*

Leona (Latin) lion. Female form of Leo. *Leola, Leone, Leonelle*

Leonora form of Eleanor. *Leonore, Nora, Norah*

Leora common form of Eleanor.

Leoti (American Indian) prairie flower.

Leslie (Scottish Gaelic) from the gray fortress. *Lesley, Lesli, Lesly, Lezlie*

Letitia (Latin) joy. *Latashia, Latia, Leisha, Leshia, Tisha*

Levana (Hebrew) moon; white. *Levania, Levona*

Levina (Latin) flash of lightning.

Lian (Chinese) graceful willow. *Leane, Lianne*

Liana (French) to bind; to wrap around. *Lianna*

Libby common form of Elizabeth. *Lib, Libbe, Libbey*

Lida (Slavic) beloved of the people.

Lila short form of Dalila; Delilah; Lillian.

Lilac (Persian) lilac flower; blue-purple.

Lilith (Arabic) of the night. First wife of Adam. *Lillis, Lilly, Lily*

Lilla (African) to ascend, to climb.

Lillian (Latin) lily flower. *Lilia, Liliane, Lilli*

Lily (Latin) lily flower. Common form of Lilith; Lillian. *Lil, Lili, Lilli, Lillie, Lilly*

Lina short form of names ending in -leen , -lena, -lene, -lina, and -line.

Linda (Spanish) pretty. Short form of names ending in -linda. *Lindi, Lyndy*

Lindsay, Lindsey (Old English) from the linden tree island.

Linette (Celtic) graceful; (Old French) linnet (bird). *Lana, Lynn, Lynette*

Lipsha (Hebrew) love, beloved. *Lipshe*

Lisa common form of Elizabeth. Short form of names ending in -lisa or -lise. *Leeza, Lise, Lisette*

Lisha (Arabic) the darkness before midnight.

Liza common form of Elizabeth. *Lizette, Lizzie*

Lois form of Louise.

Lola common form of Dolores; Louise.

Lolita (Spanish) common form of Lola. *Lita*

Lona (Middle English) solitary. *Lonee, Loni*

Lora, Lori forms of Laura. *Loria, Lorianna, Lorianne*

Lorelei (German) alluring. Sirens of the river Rhine. *Loralee, Loralie, Loralyn, Lorilee, Lorilyn, Lura, Lurette, Lurleen, Lurlene, Lurline*

Lorelle (Latin/Old German) little.

Loretta common form of Laura.

Lorraine (French) from the town Lorraine. *Lara, Laura, Laraine, Lori*

Lottie short form of Charlotte. *Lona, Lotte*

Lotus (Greek) Lotus flower.

Lou short form of Louella; Louise.

Louise (Old German) famous woman warrior. Female form of Louis. *Eloise, Lois, Louisa, Lulu*

Luana (Old German/Hebrew) graceful woman warrior. *Louanne, Luane*

Lucille common form of Lucy. *Lucila, Lucilla*

Lucinda common form of Lucy. *Cindy, Lucky*

Lucretia (Latin) riches' reward. *Lucrece*

Lucy (Latin) light; light-bringer. Female form of Lucius; Luke. *Lu, Luce, Luci, Lucia, Lucienne, Lucilla, Lucille, Lucina, Lucinda, Lucine*

Lulu (African) a pearl.

Luna (Latin) moon.
Lunette

Lurleen, Lurlene
modern forms of Lorelei.

Lydia (Greek) from Lydia.
Lidia, Lydie

Lynn (Old English)
waterfall; pool below a
fall. Short form of names
containing lin, line, or
lyn. *Lin, Linell, Linn,
Linnell, Lyn, Lyndel,
Lyndell, Lynelle, Lynette,
Lynna, Lynne, Lynnell,
Lynnelle, Lynnett, Lynnette*

M

Mabel (Latin) lovable. *Mabelle, Maybelle.*

Macawi (American Indian) generous; motherly.

Macha (American Indian) aurora.

Machi (Japanese) ten thousand thousand (a wish for long-life).

Madeline (Greek) Magdalene, woman from Magdala. *Dalenna, Maddie, Madlen, Maidel, Marlene, Maude*

Madge common form of Madeline; Margaret.

Mae form of May.

Maeve form of Mauve.

Mabel (Latin) lovable. *Mab, Maybelle*

Mackenzie (Irish Gaelic) son of the wise leader. *Kenzie*

Magda (Hebrew) woman of Magdala.

Magdalena (Greek) tower. *Magda*

Magena (American Indian) the coming moon. *Magen*

Maggie common form of Margaret. *Maggee*

Mahalia (Hebrew) affection. *Mahala*

Mai (Japanese) brightness.

Maia (Greek) mother or nurse; goddess of springtime. *Maiah, Maya*

Maida (Old English) maiden. *Madeline, Mady, Magda, Maidie*

Maile (Hawaiian) myrtle vine.

Maisie common form of Margaret. *Maisey*

Maizah (African) discerning.

Makana (Hawaiian) gift; present.

Makda (Ethiopian) woman from Magdala.

Malak (African) angel.

Malila (American Indian) salmon going fast up a rippling stream.

Malka (Hebrew) queen. *Malkah*

Mallory (French) the mailed (referring to a knight's armor). *Malorie, Malory*

Mamie common form of Margaret.

Manda (Spanish) battle maiden. *Mandy*

Mandy common form of Amanda. *Manda; Melinda.*

Manuela (Spanish) God is with us. Female form of Emmanuel.

Mapuana (Hawaiian) wind-blown fragrance.

Mara form of Mary. Short form of Amara; Damara.

Marcella (Latin) belonging to Mars; warlike. Female form of Mark. *Marcelle, Marcy*

Marcia (Latin) warlike. Female form of Mark. *Marcille, Marsha*

Marcie, Marcy common forms of Marcella; Marcia. *Marci*

Margaret (Greek) pearl. *Gretchen, Madge, Margareta, Margery, Marget, Margette, Margit, Marjorie, Marketa, Meghan*

Margery common form of Margaret. *Marge, Marjorie*

Margo, Margot (French) common forms of Margaret. *Margaux, Margeaux*

Marguerite (French) form of Margaret.

Maria form of Mary. *Mareah, Mariya*

Marian combination of Mary + Ann. *Mariana, Maryann, Miriam*

Maribel combination of Mary + Belle. *Maribelle, Marybelle, Mirabel*

Marie (French) form of Mary. *Mari*

Mariel (Dutch) form of Mary. *Mariele, Marielle*

Marietta common form of Mary.

Marilla (Hebrew/Old German) Mary of the fine mind.

Marilyn common form of Mary. *Marilee, Marilin, Marlene, Marylin, Merry*

Marina (Latin) from the sea. *Marinna, Maris, Marne, Marni*

Maris (Latin) of the sea. Short form of Damara. *Marina, Marisa, Marris, Mary*

Marissa form of Maris.

Marjorie form of Margery.

Marlene form of Madeline. *Marilyn, Marla, Marlane, Marlee, Marleen, Marlena, Marley, Marlyn, Marna*

Marlo form of Mary.

Marnie common form of Marina. *Marlene, Marna, Marney*

Marsha form of Marcia.

Martha (Aramaic) lady. Biblical sister of Mary. *Marta, Martelle, Marthe, Marthena, Marti, Martie, Martina, Martita, Marty, Martynne, Matti, Mattie, Matty, Pat, Patti, Pattie, Patty*

Mary (Hebrew) bitter. Mother of Jesus. *Maire, Malia, Manya, Marice, Marilee, Marin, Marita, Marnia, Maura, Mavra, Minette, Moira, Murial*

Maryann form of Marian. *Maryanna*

Marybeth combination of Mary + Beth. *Maribeth*

Maryellen combination of Mary + Ellen. *Mariellen*

Maryjo combination of Mary + Joan. *Marijo*

Marylou combination of Mary + Louise. *Meryl*

Mashavu (African) baby with chubby cheeks.

Matilda (Old German) powerful in battle. *Matti, Maud, Tillie*

Mattie, Matty short forms of Matilda.

Maud, Maude common forms of Madeline; Matilda. *Maudie*

Maura (Irish) form of Mary

Mawusi (African) in the hands of God.

Maureen (Old French) dark-skinned; (Irish) Common form of Mary. Female form of Maurice. *Maura, Maurine, Maurita, Moira, Morena*

Maxine (Latin) greatest. Female form of Max. *Max, Maxi*

May (Latin) great; Maia was goddess of springtime. *Mae, Maia, Mei*

Mead, Meade (Greek) honey wine.

Meara (Irish Gaelic) mirth.

Meg common form of Margaret; Megan.

Megan (Greek) great; (Irish) form of Margaret. *Meg, Megen, Meggie*

Mei (Chinese) beautiful; plum; sister; rose.

Melanie (Greek) dark-clothed. *Mel, Mellie, Milena*

Melba (Greek) soft; slender. Female form of Melvin. *Malva, Melva*

Melina (Latin) canary; yellow-colored. *Madeline, Melinda.*

Melinda (Greek) dark, gentle. *Linda, Linnie, Malinda, Mandy*

Melisande (French) common form of Melissa; Millicent. *Lisandra, Melisandra*

Melissa (Greek) honey bee. *Melessa, Melise, Melita, Melly, Milly, Misha*

Melody (Greek) song. *Melodie*

Melvina (Celtic) like a chieftain. Female form of Melvin. *Malvina, Melva*

Mercedes (Spanish) mercies.

Mercy (Middie English) compassion, mercy. *Merci, Mercie*

Meredith (Welsh) guardian from the sea. *Merridie, Merry*

Meriel common form of Muriel.

Merle (Latin/French) blackbird. *Merlina, Merola,*

Merry (Middle English) merry. Short form of Meredith. *Merrie, Merrile, Merrilee*

Mia (Italian) mine, my. Common form of Michelle

Micaela (Hebrew) who is like God. *Michaila, Michla*

Michael (Hebrew) who is like the Lord. *Micah, Michelle, Mychael*

Michelle (Hebrew) who is like the Lord. Female form of Michael. *Mia, Michaela, Michele, Michelina, Micheline, Michell, Micki, Mikaela, Misha, Miquela*

Michiko (Japanese) the righteous way. *Miche, Michi*

Mildred (Old English) gentle counselor. *Milli, Millie, Milly*

Millicent (Old German) industrious. Form of Melissa. *Lissa, Melisande, Milly, Millie*

Millie, Milly short forms of Camille; Emily; Melissa; Mildred; Millicent.

Mimi (French) common form of Miriam.

Minda (Indian) knowledge. *Mindy*

Mindy common form of Melinda; Minna. *Mindi*

Minerva (Greek) wisdom. Goddess of wisdom. *Minnie, Minny, Myna*

Minna (Old German) tender affection. Short form of Wilhelmina. *Minetta, Minnie, Minta*

Minnie common form of Minerva; Minna; Wilhelmina.

Mira (Latin) wonderful. Short form of Mirabel; Miranda. *Mirella, Mirielle, Myra, Myrilla*

Mirabel (Latin) of extraordinary beauty. *Mira, Mirabella, Mirabelle, Miranda*

Miranda (Latin) admirable. Heroine of Shakespeare's *The Tempest. Miran, Myra, Randa*

Miriam (Hebrew) bitter. Original Hebrew form of Mary. *Mimi, Mitzi*

Missy common form of Melissa; Millicent.

Misty (Old English) covered with a mist.

Mitzi common form of Miriam.

Mitsu (Japanese) light. *Mitsuko*

Miyoko (Japanese) beautiful generation child.

Modesty (Latin) modest. *Modesta, Modestine*

Modupe (African) I am grateful.

Moira (Irish Gaelic) great. Form of Mary. *Maura, Maureen.*

Mollie, Molly (Irish) common forms of Mary. *Mollee*

Mona (Greek) solitary; (Irish Gaelic) noble. Short form of Monica. *Moina, Monah, Myrna*

Monica (Latin) advisor. *Mona, Monique*

Moon (Korean) learned.

Morgana (Welsh) edge of the sea. Female form of Morgan. *Morgan, Morganica, Morgen*

Moriah (Hebrew) God is my teacher.

Mosi (African) the first-born.

Mugamba (African) name give to people who talk too much.

Muireann (Irish) of the long hair. *Morrin*

Murasaki (Japanese) purple.

Muriel (Arabic) myrrh; (Irish Gaelic) sea-bright. Form of Mary. *Meriel, Murielle*

Mu lan (Chinese) magnolia blossom. *Mu tan*

Mwasaa (African) timely.

Myfanawy (Welsh) my fine one.

Myra (Old French) quiet song. Form of Mira; Miranda.

Myrna (Irish Gaelic) polite; gentle. *Merna, Mirna, Moina, Mona, Morna, Moyna*

Myrtle (Greek) myrtle. *Myrta, Myrtia, Myrtice, Myrtie*

Myung (Korean) brightness.

N

Naamit (Hebrew) bird.

Naavah (Hebrew) beautiful.

Nada ((French/Slavic) hope. Form of Nadine. (African) generosity; dew. *Nadia, Nadine*

Nadine (French/Slavic) hope. Female form of Nathan. *Nada, Nadia, Nadiya, Nady, Nadya*

Nailah (African) one who succeeds.

Nalani (Hawaiian) the heavens.

Nan common form of Ann. *Nana, Nancy, Nanette, Nanice, Nanine, Netty*

Naomi (Hebrew) pleasant. Biblical of Ruth. *Naoma, Nomi*

Nara (American Indian, Japanese) oak.

Nari (Japanese) thunderclap. *Nariko*

Natalie (Latin) Christmas; born on Christmas day. *Natala, Natalina, Natasha, Natty, Noel*

Natasha (Russian) common form of Natalie. *Nastassia*

Neda (Slavic) born on Sunday. Female form of Edward. *Nedda, Nedi*

Neema (African) born during prosperous times.

Nelia short form of Cornelia. *Neely*

Nell common form of Cornelia; Eleanor. *Nellie, Nelly*

Nam (Korean) south.

Nani (Hawaiian) beautiful.

Nayo (African) we have joy.

Nerissa (Greek) of the sea. *Nerita*

Nessie common form of Agnes.

Neva (Spanish) snowy. *Nevada*

Nguyet (Vietnamese) moon.

Nicole (Greek) victory of the people. Female form of Nicholas. *Colette, Nickie, Nicol, Nicolette, Nikolia*

Nikki common form of Nicole.

Nina (Spanish) girl. Common form of Ann. *Ninetta, Ninon*

Nissa (Scandinavian) friendly elf or brownie. *Nisse, Nissie, Nissy*

Nita (American Indian) bear; (Spanish) common form of Ann (from Juanita).

Nituna (American Indian) my daughter.

Noel (Latin/French) born on Christmas day. *Natalie, Noella, Noellyn, Novelia*

Nohea (Hawaiian) loveliness.

Nola (Latin) small bell; (Irish) form of Olivia. *Nolana*

Nona (Latin) the ninth. One of the three Fates. *Nonah, Noni*

Nora, Norah short form of Eleanor.

Noreen (Irish) common form of Norma. *Norine*

Novia (Latin) newcomer; (Spanish) sweetheart. *Nova*

Nu (Vietnamese) girl.

Nuna (American Indian) land.

Nur (African) light. *Nuru*

Nuwa (Chinese) mother goddess.

Nyssa (Greek) beginning.

O

Octavia (Latin) eighth; eighth child. Female form of Octavius. _Octavie, Tavia_

Ode (African) born along the road.

Odelia (Hebrew) I will praise God; (Old Anglo/French) little and wealthy. Female form of Odell. _Odelinda, Odetta, Othilia, Uta_

Odetta form of Odelia.

Odina (American Indian) mountain.

Ofra (Hebrew) young deer.

Okalani (Hawaiian) of the heavens.

Oksana (Russian) praise be to God. _Ksana, Ksanochka, Oksanochka_

Olabisi (African) joy is multiplied.

Olathe (American Indian) beautiful.

Olethea (Latin) truth. _Alethea, Oleta_

Olga (Scandinavian) holy. _Elga, Helga, Olivia_

Oliana (Polynesian) oleander.

Olinda (Old German) protector of property.

Olivia (Latin) olive tree; (English) form of Olga. _Liva, Nola, Olga, Olivette_

Olympia (Greek) heavenly.

Omaira (Arabic) red.

Omolara (African) born at the right time.

Ona form of Una. _Oona_

Onaona (Hawaiian) sweet fragrance.

Ondine (Latin) wave wavelet. _Undine_

Oneida, Onida (American Indian) expected.

Onzia (African) bad.

Oona (Irish) form of Una.

Opal (Hindu) precious stone. *Opalina*

Ophelia (Greek) serpent. *Filia, Phelia*

Oralee (Hebrew) my light. *Arali, Orlee*

Oralie (French) form of Aurelia.

Orenda (American Indian) magic powers.

Oriana (Latin) dawn; golden. *Oriane*

Oriel golden.

Oriole (Latin) fair-haired. *Oriel*

Ortrud (Teutonic) serpent-maid.

Orva (Old French) of golden worth; courageous friend.

Ottilia (Old German) lucky heroine.

Ozigbodi (African) patience.

Ozlem (Turkish) longing, ardent desire.

P

Page (French) useful assistant.

Paige (Old English) child; young.

Paka (African) pussycat.

Palila (Hawaiian) bird.

Palma (Latin) palm tree. *Palmer, Palmira*

Paloma (Spanish) dove.

Pamela (Greek) all-honey. *Pam, Pamelina, Pammy*

Pandora (Greek) all-gifted.

Pansy (Greek) fragrant. *Pansie*

Panya (Latin) crowned with laurel. Form of Stephania.

Panyin (African) eldest of twins.

Pasua (African) born by Caesarean operation.

Patience (French) enduring expectation.

Patricia (Latin) of the nobility. Female form of Patrick. *Patrice, Patsy, Patty, Trish*

Patsy, Patti, Patty short forms of Patricia.

Paula (Latin) small. Female form of Paul. *Paolina, Pauletta, Paulita, Polly*

Paulette common form of Paula.

Pauline common form of Paula. *Paulina*

Pazi (American Indian) yellow bird.

Pazit (Hebrew) golden. *Pazia, Pazice, Paz, Paza*

Peace (Middle English) the peaceful.

Pearl (Latin) pearl. *Pearline, Perla, Perry*

Peg, Peggy common forms of Margaret (from Meg).

Pelagia (Greek) the sea. *Pelage*

Penny short form of Penelope. *Pennie*

Perry (French) pear tree; (Welsh) son of Harry. Common form of Pearl.

Pessa (Hebrew) pearl. *Pessel, Pessye, Pesha, Peshe*

Petra (Greek/Latin) rock. Female form of Peter. *Petrina*

Petronela (Greek) stone.

Petula (Latin) seeker. *Petulah*

Petunia (American Indian) petunia flower.

Philana (Greek) lover of mankind. Female form of Philander.

Penelope (Greek) weaver. *Penny*

Philippa (Greek) lover of horses. Female form of Philip. *Philly, Pippy*

Philomena (Greek) loving song. *Mena*

Phoebe (Greek) shining.

Phyllis (Greek) green bough.

Pia (Italian) devout.

Pilar (Spanish) pillar. Religious names of the Virgin Mary.

Pilis (Greek) lover of horses.

Ping (Chinese) duckweed; (Vietnamese) peace.

Piper (Old English) player of the pipe.

Pippa, Pippy common forms of Philippa.

Placidia (Latin) the serene. *Placida*

Polly common form of Molly; Paula.

Pollyanna Combination of Polly + Ann.

Pomona (Latin) fertile; apple. Goddess of fruit trees.

Poppy (Latin) poppy flower.

Portia (Latin) offering. *Porche, Porsha*

Prima (Latin) first; first child.

Priscilla (Latin) from ancient times. *Prisca, Prissie*

Prudence (Latin) foresight; intelligence. *Prudy, Prue*

Prunella (Latin) brown. *Prue, Nella*

Pua (Hawaiian) flower.

Pualani (Hawaiian) heavenly flower. *Punani*

Purity (Middle English) purity.

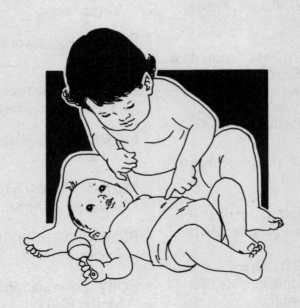

Q

Qadira (Arabic) powerful. *Kadira*

Qamra (Arabic) moon. *Kamra*

Qiànrú (Chinese) nice smile.

Qiturah (Arabic) fragrance.

Qubilah (African) concord.

Queenie (Latin) form of Regina; queen. *Queen*

Quenby (Scandinavian) womanly.

Querida (Spanish) beloved.

Questa (French) searcher.

Quiana (Hebrew) gracious. Form of Anna.

Quinn (Old English) queen.

Quinta (Latin) five; fifth child. Female form of Quentin. *Quentin, Quintina*

Quintessa (Latin) essence. *Tess, Tessa*

R

Raananah (Hebrew) fresh.

Rachel (Hebrew) ewe; a female sheep. *Rae, Raquel, Rey, Shelly*

Rae (Old English) doe. Common form of Rachel. *Raeann, Ralina, Rayna*

Rabab (Arabic) white cloud.

Radeyah (Arabic) content; satisfied.

Ragner (Scandinavian) god's lovely gift. *Ragnhild*

Raiden (Japanese) thunder god.

Rajni (Hindi) night.

Raku (Japanese) pleasure.

Ramona (Spanish) mighty or wise protectress. Female form of Raymond. *Ramonda, Romona, Romonda*

Rana (Arabic) hope.

Randy short female form of Randall; Randolph. *Randa, Randene*

Rani (Hindi) queen. *Rana, Ranee, Ranice*

Ranit (Hebrew) song. *Ranita, Ranitta*

Raphaela (Hebrew) blessed healer. Female form of Raphael. *Rafa*

Raquel (Spanish) form of Rachel.

Rashida (African) righteous. *Rashidi*

Raven (Old English) like the raven.

Raziya (African) agreeable.

Reba short form of Rebecca. (Hebrew) fourth-born.

Rebecca (Hebrew) wife of Isaac. *Beckie, Becky, Rebecka, Riva*

Regan (English) form of Regina.

Regina (Latin) queen. *Raina, Regan, Rina*

Reiko (Japanese) gratitude; propriety.

Rena (Hebrew) song. *Reena, Rina, Rinna, Rinah*

Renata (Latin) reborn. *Renae*

Rene short form of Irene; Renée. *Renie*

Rene (French) from Renata. *Renell, Renelle*

Reta (African) to shake. *Rhetta*

Reyhan (Turkish) sweet smelling flower.

Rezi (Greek/Hungarian) harvester. From Tereza. *Riza*

Rhea (Greek) earth; that which flows from the earth as rivers. *Rea*

Rhoda (Greek) roses; from Rhodes. Form of Rose. *Rhodie, Roda, Rodina*

Rhona form of Rona. *Roana*

Rhonda name of southern Wales grand. *Ronda*

Ria (Spanish) mouth of the river.

Riane female form of Ryan. *Ryann*

Rica common form of Frederica. *Ricca, Rikki*

Ricarda (Old German) powerful ruler. Female form of Richard. *Richarda*

Richelle female form of Richard. *Richela*

Richia female form of Richard.

Ricki, Rickie short forms of Frederica; Rica.

Rihana (Muslim) sweet basil. *Rhiana, Riana*

Ringo (Japanese) apple; peace be with you.

Risa (Latin) laughter.

Rita short form of
Margaret; from
Margherita.

Riva (French) shore. Short
form of Rebecca. *Rivalee,
Rivi*

Rivka (Hebrew) God's
servant. *Rebecca, Riva,
Rive*

Roanna form of
Rosanne. *Ranna, Roanne,
Ronni, Ronnie, Ronny*

Roberta (Old English)
shining with fame.
Female form of Robert.
*Bobbie, Bobina, Robena,
Robin, Robina, Ruperta*

Robin, Robyn (Old
English) robin. Common
form of Roberta. *Robbi,
Robbyn, Robinett, Robinia*

Rochelle (French) from
the little rock. Form of
Rachel. *Rochette, Shelley*

Roderica (Old German)
famous ruler. Female
form of Roderick. *Rica*

Rohana (Hindi)
sandalwood.

Rolanda (Old German)
fame of the land. Female
form of Roland.

Roma (Latin) eternal city.
Romelle, Romina

Rona (Scandinavian)
mighty power; mighty
runner. Female form of
Ronald.

Ronit (Hebrew) joy is
mine. *Rona, Ronia, Ronli*

Rosabel combination of
Rose + Belle. *Rosabella*

Rosalba (Latin) white
rose.

Rosalie (Irish) common
form of Rose. *Rosalia,
Rozele*

Rosalind (Spanish)
beautiful rose. *Rosalyn,
Roselin, Roslyn*

Rosalyn combination of
Rose + Lynn. Form of
Rosalind.

Rosamond (Old German) famous guardian. *Ros, Rosmunda, Rosemonde*

Rose (Greek) rose. *Rosalie, Roselle, Rosetta, Rosina, Rozella, Zita*

Rosemariá (Spanish) combination of Rose + Mary.

Roseanne combination of Rose + Ann. *Roanna, Rosanne, Rozanna*

Roselani (Hawaiian) heavenly rose.

Rosemary (Latin) rosemary (the herb). *Rosemaria, Rosemarie*

Rowena (Celtic) white mane; (Old English) well-known friend. *Rena, Ronnie, Rowe*

Roxanne (Persian) dawn. *Rosana, Roxanna, Roxie, Roxy*

Ruby (Old French) ruby. *Rubetta, Rubia*

Rúfen (Chinese) nice fragrance.

Rufina (Latin) red hair.

Ruri (Japanese) emerald. *Ruriko*

Rukiya (African) she rises on high.

Ruth (Hebrew) friend of beauty. *Ruthie*

Ruthann combination of Ruth + Ann.

Ryu (Japanese) lofty.

Ryung (Korean) brightness.

S

Sabah (African) morning.

Sabina (Latin) Sabine woman; woman from Sheba. *Sheba, Brina, Sabine, Savina*

Sabra (Hebrew) thorny cactus. Name for a native-born Israeli girl.

Sabirah (African) patient.

Sabrina (Latin) from the boundary line. *Brina, Zabrina*

Sachi (Japanese) bliss child; joy. *Sachiko*

Sadie common form of Sarah. *Sada, Saidee, Sydelle*

Sakura (Japanese) cherry blossom.

Salena (Latin) salty. *Salina*

Salimah (African) healthy; safe.

Sally common form of Sal. *Sallee, Salli, Sallie*

Salome (Hebrew) peace. *Saloma, Salome, Salomi*

Samala (Hebrew) asked of God. *Samale*

Samantha (Aramaic) listener. *Sam, Sammy*

Samara (Hebrew) ruled by God. *Sam, Samaria, Sammy*

Sandra short form of Alexandra. *Sandi, Sandy, Sandye, Zandra*

Sandy common form of Sandra. *Sandi, Sandie, Sandye*

Sapphire (Greek) sapphire stone; sapphire blue. *Sapphira, Sephira*

Sara (English) form of Sarah.

Sarah (Hebrew) princess. Wife of Abraham and mother of Isaac. *Sadella, Sallee, Sarena, Sari, Sarita, Shari, Sharon, Sharona, Sherri, Zarah*

Saree (Arabic) most noble. *Sari*

Sasha (Russian) common form of Alexandra. *Sacha, Sascha, Sashenka*

Savanna (Spanish) barren one.

Scarlett (Middle English) scarlet. Heroine of *Gone with the Wind.*

Seema (Hebrew) treasure. *Cyma, Sima*

Seiko (Japanese) force; truth. *Sei*

Selena (Greek) moon. *Celina, Celinda, Seline, Sena*

Selima (Hebrew) peaceful. Female form of Solomon.

Selma (Scandinavian) divinely protected. Female form of Anselm. *Anselma, Zelma*

Senalda (Spanish) a sign. *Sena*

Seraphina (Hebrew) burning ardent. Highest order of angels. *Serafina, Serafine, Seraphine*

Serena (Latin) calm; serene. *Reena, Rena, Sarina, Serene*

Shaina (Hebrew) beautiful. *Shaine, Shayna*

Shana common form of Shannon.

Shani (African) marvelous.

Shannon (Irish Gaelic) small; wise. *Channa, Shana, Shani, Shanon, Shawna*

Shari (Hungarian) form of Sarah.

Sharon (Hebrew) plain. Form of Sarah. *Shara, Sharona, Sherrie*

Shawn Female form of John. *Sean, Seana, Shawnee, Sianna*

Sheba (Hebrew) from the Sheba. *Saba*

Shea (Irish Gaelic) from the fairy fort. *Shayla, Shaylynn*

Sheena (Irish) form of Jane.

Sheila (Irish) form of Cecilia. *Selia, Shela, Shelia*

Shelby (Old English) from the ledge estate. *Shel, Shellie*

Shelley (Old English) from the meadow on the ledge. Common form of Rachel; Sheila; Shelby; Shirley.

Sherry common form of Charlotte; Cher; Sarah

Sheryl common form of Shirley. *Sherilyn*

Shifra (Hebrew) beautiful. *Schifra, Shifrah*

Shina (Japanese) good; virtue. *Sheena*

Shira (Hebrew) song. *Shiri*

Shirley (Old English) from the bright meadow. *Sherill, Sherline, Shirleen*

Shoshana (Hebrew) rose. Form of Susan.

Shulamit (Hebrew) peaceful. *Shulamith, Sula*

Sibyl (Greek) prophetess. *Cybil, Sibella, Sibelle*

Silvia form of Sylvia. *Silvie*

Simcha (Hebrew) joy.

Simone (Hebrew) one who hears. Female form of Simon. *Simona, Simonette*

Sisi (African) born on Sunday.

Skylar, Skyler (Dutch) sheltering. *Skye, Skyla*

Solana (Spanish) sunshine. *Solenne*

Sondra short form of Alexandra.

Sonia (Slavic/Scandinavian) form of Sophie. *Sonya, Sunny*

Sonnie, Sonny common forms of Sonia.

Sook (Korean) purity.

Sophie (Greek) wisdom. *Sonia, Sonny, Sophia, Sunny*

Spring (Old English) springtime.

Stacy short form of Anastasia. *Stace, Stacee, Stacey, Staci, Stacia, Stacie*

Star (English) star. *Starlene, Starr*

Stella (Latin) star. Short form of Estelle.

Stephanie (Greek) crowned. Female form of Stephen. *Stafani, Stephana, Stesha, Stevana*

Storm (Old English) stormy. *Stormie, Stormy*

Subira (African) patience rewarded.

Sue short form of Susan.

Suletu (American Indian) to fly around.

Summer (Old English) summer. *Sommer*

Sun (Korean) obedience.

Sunny (English) bright, cheerful. Common form of Sonia. *Sunshine*

Susan (Hebrew) lily. *Sosanna, Sukey, Susanetta, Susannah, Suzette, Suzie, Zsa Zsa*

Susanna, Susannah forms of Susan.

Susie, Susy short forms of Susan.

Suzanne form of Susan.

Sydney (Old French) from the city of St. Denis.

Sukey common form of Susan. *Sydel, Sydelle, Suki*

Sying (Chinese) star.

Sylvia (Latin) from the forest. *Silva, Silvana, Silvia*

T

Tabitha (Aramaic) gazelle. *Tabatha, Tabbi, Tabita*

Tacita (Latin) to be silent. *Tacy*

Taffy (Welsh) beloved.

Taima (American Indian) crash of thunder.

Talia (Greek) blooming. Greek muse of comedy. *Tallia, Tally, Talyah*

Taliba (African) seeker after knowledge.

Tallulah (American Indian) leaping water. *Tallie, Tallou, Tally*

Tamar (Hebrew) palm tree. *Tamara, Tamera, Tammie*

Tami (Japanese) people. *Tamiko*

Tani (Japanese) valley.

Tansy (Greek) immortality; (Latin) tenacious; persistent. *Tandi, Tandie, Tandy*

Tanya (Slavic) meaning unknown. *Tatiana*

Tao (Chinese) peach (symbol of long life).

Tara (Irish Gaelic) rocky pinnacle. Home of the ancient Irish kings. *Tarah, Tarra*

Taryn form of Tara. *Taran, Tareyn, Tarryn*

Tasha common form of Natasha or Anastasia. *Tawsha*

Tate (Old English) to be cheerful. *Tatum*

Tatsu (Japanese) dragon.

Taylor (Middle English) a tailor. *Tayler*

Tempest (Old French) stormy.

Teresa form of Theresa.

Terry short form of Theresa. Female form of Terence. *Tera, Teri*

Tertia (Latin) the third.

Tess short form of Tessa. Common form of Theresa. *Tessi, Tessie, Tessy*

Tessa (Greek) fourth; fourth child. Common form of Theresa. *Tess, Tessi, Tessie, Tessy*

Thalassa (Greek) from the sea.

Thalia (Greek) joyful; blooming. One of the Three Graces.

Thana (African) thankfulness.

Thea (Greek) goddess. Short form of Dorothy; Timothea.

Thelma (Greek) nursling.

Thema (African) queen.

Theodora (Greek) gift of God. Female form of Theodore. *Dora, Tedda, Teddy, Theda, Theo, Theodosia*

Theresa (Greek) reaper. *Teresita, Teressa, Tessie, Tressa, Zita*

Thomasina (Latin/Greek) little twin. Female form of Thomas. *Tammi, Thomasine, Toma, Tommie*

Thora (Scandinavian) thunder. Female form of Thor. *Thordia, Thordis, Tyra*

Tia (Greek/Egyptian) princess. Sister of the pharoah King Ramses.

Tiffany (Greek) appearance of God. *Tiff, Tiffani, Tiffanie, Tiphani*

Tilda short form of Matilda. *Tildi, Tildie, Tildy, Tilly*

Timothea (Greek) honoring God. Female form of Timothy. *Thea, Timi, Timmy*

Tina short form of names ending in -tina or -tine. *Teena, Tiena*

Tita (Latin) title of honor.

Titania (Greek) giant. Queen of the fairies in Shakespeare's *A Midsummer Night's Dream.*

Tobit (Hebrew) God is good. Female form of Tobias. *Tobe, Toby, Tova*

Tomiju (Japanese) wealth and longevity.

Tommy short form of Thomasina. *Tomi*

Toni common form of Antoinette. *Tonia, Tonle, Tony*

Tory short form of Victoria. *Torey, Tori*

Tova (Hebrew) good. *Toibe, Toba*

Tracy (Irish Gaelic) battler; (Latin)

courageous. Common form of Theresa. *Tracee, Tracey*

Tricia, Trish short forms of Patricia. *Trish*

Trina common form of Katherine. *Trenna*

Trinity (Latin) triad. *Trinidad*

Trista (Latin) melancholy. Female form of Tristan.

Trudy (Old German) beloved. Short form of Gertrude. *Truda, Trude*

Tsuhgi (Japanese) second child.

Twyla (Middle English) woven of double thread. *Twila*

Tyne (Old English) river.

Tzippa (Hebrew) bird. *Tzipporah, Sippora.*

Tziyona (Hebrew) Zion.

U

U (Korean) gentleness.

Udele (Old English) prosperous.

Ulani (Hawaiian) cheerful.

Ulrica (Old German) ruler of all. Female form of Ulric.

Ululani (Hawaiian) growing in beauty.

Umayma (African) little mother.

Umeko (Japanese) plum-tree field.

Una (Latin) one, united; (Irish) form of Agnes. Common form of Winifred. *Ona, Oona*

Urbi (African) princess.

Urika (American Indian) useful to all.

Urit (Hebrew) light. *Urice*

Ursula (Latin) little bear. *Orsa, Sula, Ursa, Ursulina*

Usi (Chinese) the ox.

Ut (Korean) last.

$\mathcal{V}$

Valda (Spanish) heroine.

Valencia (Latin) strong.

Valentina (Latin) strong; healthy. *Tina, Val, Valene, Valentine, Vallie*

Valerie (Latin) strong. *Val, Valaria, Vale, Valery, Valry*

Valora (Latin) strong, valorous. *Valorie*

Vanessa (Greek) butterfly. *Nessa, Van, Vania, Vanna, Vanny*

Varda (Hebrew) rose. *Vadit, Vardit*

Vashti (Persian) beautiful.

Veda (Sanskrit) wise. *Vedette, Veleda, Vida*

Velma common form of Wilhelmina. *Vilma*

Velvet (Middle English) velvety.

Venus (Latin) Venus; goddess of beauty. *Venita, Vin, Vinita, Vinnle, Vinny*

Vera (Latin) true; (Slavic) faith. Short form of Veronica. *Verena, Verina, Verla*

Verda (Latin) young fresh. *Verdi*

Verena (Old German) defender. Common form of Vera; Verna.

Verna (Latin) springlike. *Vernice*

Veronica (Latin/Greek) true image. Form of Bernice. *Ronica, Ronnie, Vera, Véronique*

Vicki, Vicky short forms of Victoria.

Victoria (Latin) victory. Female form of Victor. *Vicki, Vickie*

Vida short form of Davita. *Veda, Vita, Vitia*

Viet (Vietnamese) destroy.

Vitel (Hebrew) life. *Vitka, Vitke*

Viola form of Violet.

Violet (Latin) violet flower. *Vi, Viola, Violetta, Yolanda, Yolane*

Virginia (Latin) virginal maidenly. *Ginelle, Ginnie*

Vivian (Latin) full of life. *Vivi, Viviana, Vivianne, Vivien*

Volante (French) form of Violette.

Vona (French) diminutive of Yvonne.

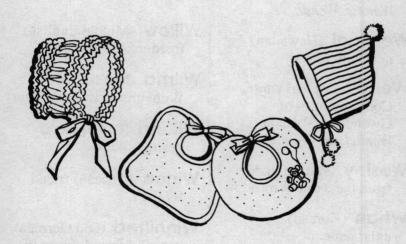

W

Wafa (Arabic) faithfulness.

Walida (Arabic) newborn.

Wallis (Old English) from Wales. Female form of Wallace. *Wallie, Wally*

Wanda (Old German) wanderer. *Wandie, Wandis, Wenda*

Wehilani (Hawaiian) heavenly robes.

Wendy (Welsh) white. Common form of Gwendolyn; Wanda. *Wendeline, Wendie*

Wesley (Old English) from the western meadow.

Whan (Korean) enlargement.

Whitney (Old English) from the white island. *Whitnie, Whittney*

Wilda (Old English) willow.

Wilhelmina (Old German) determined guardian. Female form of William. *Billie, Minna, Minni, Minnie, Willette, Wilma, Wylma*

Willa short form of Wilhelmina. Female form of William. *Willi, Willie, Willy*

Willow (Middle English) freedom; willow tree.

Wilma short form of Wilhelmina. *Valma, Vilma*

Wilona (Old English) desired. *Wilone*

Winna (African) friend. *Winnah*

Winnifred (Old German) peaceful friend. Form of Guinevere. *Freddie, Oona, Una, Wynn*

Winona (American Indian) eldest daughter. *Winnie, Winonah*

Winter (Old English) winter.

Wren (Old English) wren.

Wyanet (American Indian) beautiful.

Wynne (Welsh) fair. Short form of Gwendolyn; Gwyneth. *Winne*

X

Xaviera (Arabic) brilliant; (Spanish Basque) owner of the new house. Female form of Xavier.

Xenia (Greek) hospitable. *Xena, Zena, Zenia*

Xiu Mei (Chinese) beautiful plum.

Xuan (Vietnamese) spring.

Xylia (Greek) of the wood. *Sylvia*

Y

Yael, Ya-el (Hebrew) ascent. *Jael*

Yaffa (Hebrew) beautiful.

Yao (African) born on Thursday. *Yawo*

Yasu (Japanese) tranquil.

Yehudit (Hebrew) praise. *Judith, Judit, Judinta, Yuta*

Yesima (Hebrew) right hand; strength.

Yasmin (Arabic) jasmine.

Yetta (Old English) to give; giver. Short form of Henrietta.

Yin (Chinese) silver.

Yoki (American Indian) rain; bluebird on the mesa.

Yoko (Japanese) the positive.

Yolanda (Greek) violet flower. French form of Violet. *Yolande, Yolane*

Yonina (Hebrew) dove. *Jona, Jonina, Yona, Yonit*

Yoshiko (Japanese) good. *Yoshi*

Yuki (Japanese) snow. *Yukie*

Yvette common form of Yvonne. *Ivett, Ivette, Yevette*

Yvonne (Old French) archer. Female form of Ivar; Ives. *Evonne, Ivonne*

Z

Zafirah (African) victorious, successful.

Zahara (African) flower.

Zahra (African) white; flowers.

Zara (Hebrew) dawn. Form of Sarah. *Zarah, Zaria*

Zelda (Hebrew) rare. Short form of Griselda. *Selda, Zelde*

Zena form of Xenia. *Zenia*

Zenobia (Greek) sign symbol. *Zeba, Zena*

Zesiro (African) elder of twins.

Zetta (Hebrew) olive. *Zetana*

Zia (Latin) kind of grain. *Zea*

Zina (African) name.

Zita short form of names ending in -sita or -zita.

Ziva (Hebrew) splendor; brightness.

Zoö (Greek) life. *Zoey*

Zola (Italian) ball of earth.

Zora (Slavic) aurora dawn. *Zorah, Zorina*

Zsa Zsa (Hungarian) common form of Susan.

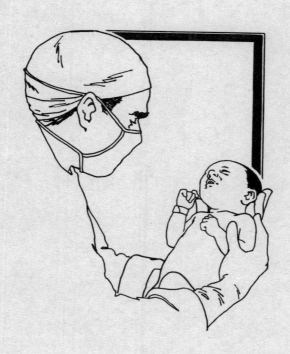

Boys' Names

A

Aaron (Hebrew) enlightened; teaching; mountaineer. *Ahron, Ari, Aron, Ron, Ronny*

Aba (African) born on Thursday.

Aban (Arabic) old, traditional Arabic name.

Abbey short form of Abbott; Abner. *Abbie, Abby*

Abbott (Hebrew) father; abbot. *Abbie*

Abd al jabbar (Arabic) servant of the Mighty.

Abdalla (African) searvant of God.

Abdul (Arabic) son of.

Abel (Hebrew) breath. Short form of Abelard; Abraham; Abram.

Abner (Hebrew) father of light. *Abbey, Abbie, Avner*

Abraham (Hebrew) father of the multitude. First Hebrew patriarch. *Abe, Abey, Abie, Abram, Avram*

Adam (Hebrew) man of the earth. First man created by God. *Adamo, Addie, Ade*

Addison (Old English) son of Adam. *Addie*

Adir (Hebrew) majestic; noble.

Adlai (Hebrew) my witness. *Ad, Addie*

Adler (Old German) eagle. *Ad*

Adolph (Old German) noble wolf; noble hero. *Adolf, Dolph*

Adriel (Hebrew) of God's majesty. *Adrial*

Afryea (African) born during good times.

Ahearn (Celtic) lord of the horses. *Ahern*

Ahmed (Arabic) most highly praised. *Ahmad*

Aidan (Irish Gaelic) warmth of the home. *Aiden*

Aitan (Hebrew) strength. *Ethan*

Akihiko (Japanese) bright male child.

Akira (Japanese) intelligent.

Al short form of names beginning with Al.

Alan (Irish Gaelic) handsome; cheerful. *Allan, Allen*

Alastair (Scottish) form of Alexander. *Al, Alistair, Alister*

Alben (Latin) fair, blond. *Al, Alban, Albie, Albin*

Albert (Old English) noble and bright. *Albie, Albrecht, Bert, Elbert*

Alcott (Old English) from the old cottage. *Alcot*

Alden (Old English) old, wise protector. *Aldin, Elden*

Aldous (Old German) old and wise. *Al, Aldis, Aldo, Aldus*

Aldrich (Old English) old, wise ruler. *Aldridge, Eldridge, Richie*

Alec, Alex short forms of Alexander.

Alena (Hawaiian) handsome; cheerful. From Alan.

Alexander (Greek) helper of mankind. Alexander the Great. *Alastair, Alejandro, Alexandre, Alister, Sander, Saunder*

Alexis common form of Alexander. *Alexi*

Alfonso (Italian) form of Alphonse.

Alfred (Old English) wise counselor. *Alfie, Alfredo, Avery, Freddie*

Alger (Old German) noble spearman. Short form of Algernon.

Algernon (Old French) bearded. *Alger, Algie*

Ali (African) exalted.

Allan, Allen forms of Alan.

Allard (Old English) noble and brave. *Al*

Alongo (African) tall and skinny boy.

Alonzo form of Alphonse. *Alonso*

Aloysius (Old German) famous in war.

Alphonse (Old German) noble and eager. *Alfie, Alonso, Fonzie*

Alton (Old English) from the old town. *Alten*

Alvin (Old German) beloved by all. *Alva, Alvan, Elvin*

Ambrose (Greek) immortal. *Ambros, Ambrosio*

Amiel (Hebrew) God of my people.

Amory form of Emery. *Amery*

Amos (Hebrew) burden. Hebrew prophet.

An (Chinese) peace; (Vietnamese) peace; safety.

Anastasius (Greek) one who shall rise again. *Anastase, Anastatius*

Anatole (Greek) man from the east. *Anatol, Anatollo*

Anders (Swedish) form of Andrew. *Anderson*

Andre (French) form of Andrew. *Andras, Andris*

Andrew (Greek) strong; manly. One of the Twelve Apostles. *Andre, Andy, Drew*

Andy short form of Andrew.

Angelo (Greek) angel. *Ange, Angell, Angie, Angy*

Angus (Scottish Gaelic) unique choice; one strength. *Ennis, Gus*

Anoki (American Indian) actor.

Ansel (Old French) adherent of a nobleman. *Ancell, Ansell*

Anson (Old German) of divine origin. *Hanson*

Anthony (Latin) priceless. *Antoine, Anton, Antony, Tony*

Antoine (French) form of Anthony.

Antonio (Italian) form of Anthony.

Archer (Old English) bowman. Short form of Archibald.

Archibald (Old German) genuinely bold. *Arch, Archibold, Archie*

Archie common form of Archer; Archibald. *Archy*

Arden (Latin) ardent fiery. *Ardin, Ardy*

Ariel (Hebrew) lion of God. *Arel, Arie*

Aristotle (Greek) the best. *Ari, Arie*

Arlen (Irish Gaelic) pledge. *Arlan, Arlin*

Armand (Old German) army man. (French) form of Herman. *Arman, Armando, Armin*

Armstrong (Old English) strong arm.

Arne (Old German) eagle. *Arney, Arnie, Arnold*

Arnie short form of Arne; Arnold.

Arnold (Old German) strong as an eagle. *Arnaud, Arney, Arnie*

Arnon (Hebrew) roaring stream.

Art, Artie short forms of Artemus; Arthur.

Artemus (Greek) gift of Artemis; safe and sound. *Artemis, Artie*

Arthur (Celtic) noble; (Welsh) bear-hero. *Art, Artie, Arturo, Artus*

Arvad (Hebrew) wanderer. *Arv, Arvid, Arvie*

Arvin (Old German) friend of the people; friend of the army. *Arv, Arvie, Arvy*

Asa (Hebrew) physician.

Asea (African) first twin to be born.

Ashby (Scandinavian) from the ash tree farm. *Ashton*

Asher (Hebrew) happy; blessed. *Ash*

Ashford (Old English) from the ash tree ford. *Ash*

Ashton (Old English) ash tree farm. *Ash, Ashley*

Aubrey (Old French) blond ruler; elf ruler. *Auberon, Avery*

Audun (Scandinavian) deserted or desolate.

August (Latin) majestic dignity. Honoring Augustus Caesar. *Augie, Augustin, Augustus, Austin, Gus*

Augustine (Latin) belonging to Augustus. Honoring St. Augustine. *Augie, Austen, Gus*

Aurelius (Latin) golden. *Aurelio*

Austin form of August; Augustine. *Austen*

Averill (Middle English) born in April. *Avery, Ave, Averell,*

Avery (English) form of Alfred; Aubrey.

Avram (Hebrew) form of Abraham; Abram.

Awan (American Indian) somebody.

Ayyub (Arabic) name of a Prophet.

Azi (African) the youth.

Azizi (African) precious.

ℬ

Babatunde (African) father loves me.

Bahir (Arabic) dazzling; brilliant.

Bailey (Old French) bailiff; steward. *Bailie*

Baird (Irish Gaelic) ballad singer. *Bard, Barde*

Bakari (African) promise.

Baldwin (Old German) bold friend.

Balfour (Scottish Gaelic) pasture land.

Bancroft (Old English) from the bean field. *Bank, Bink*

Barclay (Old English) from the birch tree meadow. *Berk, Berkley*

Bard (Irish) form of Baird. *Bar, Barr*

Barnaby (English) form of Barnabas.

Barnett (Old English) nobleman. *Barney, Barron, Barry*

Barney common form of Barnabas; Barnett; Bernard.

Baron (Old English) nobleman; baron.

Barret (Old German) mighty as a bear. *Bar, Barrett, Bear*

Barry (Irish Gaelic) spearlike; pointed; (Welsh) son of Harry. Common form of Barnett; Baruch; Bernard. *Barrie, Barris*

Bart short form of Bartholomew; Barton; Bertram.

Bartholomew (Hebrew) son of a farmer. *Bartel, Barth, Bat*

Barton (Old English) from the barley farm. *Bart, Bartie, Barty*

Bartram form of Bertram.

Baruch (Hebrew) blessed. *Barry*

Basil (Latin) magnificent; kingly. *Base, Basilius, Vassily*

Baxter (Old English) baker. *Bax*

Bayard (Old English) having reddish-brown hair. *Bay*

Beau (Old French) handsome. Short form of Beauregard. *Beale, Bo*

Beauregard (Old French) beautiful in expression. *Beau, Bo*

Bellamy (Old French) beautiful friend. *Belamy, Bell*

Ben (Hebrew) son. Short form of names beginning with Ben. *Bennie*

Ben-ami (Hebrew) son of my people.

Benedict (Latin) blessed. *Ben, Benito, Bennie, Benoit*

Benjamin (Hebrew) son of the right hand. *Ben, Benjamen, Benjie, Jamie, Jim*

Benson (Hebrew/English) son of Benjamin. *Ben, Bennie*

Bentley (Old English) from the moor. *Ben, Benny, Bentlee*

Benton (Old English) of the moors. *Ben, Bent*

Bergren (Scandinavian) mountain stream. Berg

Berkeley form of Barclay. *Berk, Berkley*

Bern (Old German) bear. Short form of Bernard. *Berne, Bernie, Bjorn*

Bernard (Old German) brave bear. *Barnard, Barney, Bernardo, Bernie*

Bert (Old English) bright. Short form of names containing bert. *Bertie, Burt, Butch*

Berthold (Old German) brilliant ruler. *Bert, Bertold*

Bertram (Old English) glorious raven. *Bart, Bert, Berton, Berty*

Bevan (Irish Gaelic) son of Evan. *Bev, Bevin*

Bill, Billy common forms of William. *Billie*

Bimisi (American Indian) slippery.

Bing (Old German) kettle-shaped hollow.

Bjorn (Scandinavian) form of Bern.

Blaine (Irish Gaelic) thin; lean. *Blane, Blayne*

Blair (Irish Gaelic) from the plain; (French) Form of Blaze.

Blake (Old English) fair-haired and fair-complected.

Blaze (Latin) stammerer. *Blaise*

Bo (American) form of Beau. Short form of Beauregard; Bogart.

Boas (Hebrew) swift; strong.

Bob, Bobby common forms of Robert. *Bobbie*

Bogart (Old French) strong as a bow. *Bo, Bogey*

Bobo (African) born on Tuesday.

Bond (Old English) tiller of the soil.

Bon-Hwa (Korean) utmost glory.

Boone (Old French) good.

Booth (Old English) from the hut. *Boothe*

Borden (Old English) from the valley of the boar. *Bord, Bordie, Bordy*

Borg (Scandinavian) from the castle.

Boris (Slavic) battler; warrior.

Boseda (African) born on a Sunday.

Botan (Japanese) peony; flower of June.

Bowie (Irish Gaelic) yellow-haired. *Bow, Bowen, Boyd*

Boyce (Old French) from the woodland. *Boy, Boycie*

Boyd (Irish) form of Bowie.

Brad (Old English) broad. Short form of names beginning with Brad.

Braden (Old English) from the wide valley. *Bradan*

Bradford (Old English) from the broad river crossing. *Brad, Ford*

Bradley (Old English) from the broad meadow. *Brad, Leigh*

Bradshaw (Old English) large virginal forest.

Brady (Irish Gaelic) spirited; (Old English) from the broad island.

Bram (Irish Gaelic) raven; (Old English) fierce; famous. Short form of Abraham; Abram.

Bramwell (Old English) of Abraham's well. *Bram*

Brand (Old English) firebrand. Short form of Brandon. *Brander, Brandy*

Brandon (Old English) from the beacon hill. *Bran, Brand, Branden, Brannon*

Brendan (Irish Gaelic) little raven. *Bren, Brendin, Brendon, Brennen, Bryn*

Brenton (Old English) from the steep hill. *Brent*

Bret, Brett (Celtic) Briton. *Brit, Britt*

Brewster (Old English) brewer. *Brew, Brewer, Bruce*

Brian (Irish Gaelic) strength; virtue. *Briano, Brien, Bryan, Bryon*

Brice form of Price. *Bryce*

Brigham (Old English) from the enclosed bridge. *Brig, Brigg, Briggs*

Brock (Old English) badger.

Broderick (Old English) from the broad ridge. *Brod, Broderic, Rick*

Bronson (Old English) son of the dark-skinned one. *Bronnie, Sonny*

Brook (Old English) from the brook. *Brooke, Brooks*

Bruce (Old French) from the brushwood thicket. *Brucie*

Bruno (Italian) brown-haired.

Bryan, Bryant form of Brian.

Bryce form of Brice.

Buck (Old English) buck deer. *Buckie, Bucky*

Bud (Old English) herald; messenger. *Budd, Buddie, Buddy*

Burgess (Old English) citizen of a fortified town. *Burr*

Burke (Old French) from the fortress. *Berk, Berke, Burk*

Burl (Old English) cup-bearer. *Burlie, Byrle*

Burne (Old English) from the brook. *Burn*

Burt form of Bert. Short form of Burton.

Burton (Old English) from the fortress. *Burt*

Buu (Vietnamese) principle; guide.

Byarugaba (African) for, by, or of God. *Byaruhanga*

Byrd (Old English) bird-like. *Byrdie*

Byron (Old French) from the cottage. *Biron, Byram, Byran*

C

Cable (Old French) rope.

Cado (Celtic) war. *Cato*

Caesar (Latin) long-haired; emperor. *César, Cesare*

Cal short form of names beginning with Cal.

Calder (Old English) stream. *Cal*

Caldwell (Old English) dweller by the cold spring. *Cal*

Caleb (Hebrew) bold one; dog. *Cal, Kaleb*

Calhoun (Celtic) warrior.

Calvert (Old English) herdsman. *Cal, Calbert*

Calvin (Latin) bald. *Cal, Kalvin, Vin, Vinny*

Camden (Scottish Gaelic) from the winding valley.

Cameron (Scottish Gaelic) crooked nose. *Cam*

Campbell (Scottish Gaelic) crooked mouth. *Cam, Camp*

Carey (Welsh) from near the castle. *Care, Cary*

Carl (Old German) farmer; (Swedish) form of Charles. Short form of names beginning with Carl.

Carleton (Old English) farmer's town. *Carl, Carlton, Charlton*

Carlin (Irish Gaelic) little champion. *Carl, Carling*

Carlisle (Old English) from the fortified town. *Carl, Carlie, Carly, Carlyle*

Carlos (Spanish) form of Charles. *Carlo*

Carmine (Latin) song.

Carney (Irish Gaelic) victorious. *Karney, Kearney*

Carr (Scandinavian) from the marsh. *Karr, Kerr*

Carroll (Irish Gaelic) champion. Common form of Charles. *Carrol, Cary, Caryl*

Carson (Old English) son of the family on the marsh.

Carter (Old English) cart driver. *Cart*

Carver (Old English) woodcarver.

Cary short form of Carey; Carroll.

Casey (Irish Gaelic) brave. *Case*

Casper (Persian) treasurer. *Caspar, Gasper*

Cassidy (Irish Gaelic) clever. *Cass, Cassie, Cassy*

Cecil (Latin) blind. *Cecile, Cecilius*

Cedric (Old English) battle chieftain. *Rick*

Chad (Old English) warlike. Short form of names like Chadwick; Chadbourne. Common form of Charles.

Chadwick (Old English) from the warrior's town. *Chad, Chadd*

Chaim (Hebrew) life. *Chayam, Hayyim, Hyman, Manny*

Channing (Old English) knowing; (Old French) canon. *Chan, Chane, Conan*

Chapman (Old English) merchant. *Chap, Manny*

Charles (Old German) manly; strong. *Carl, Chad, Charlie, Chicky, Chuck*

Charlton form of Carleton.

Chase (Old French) hunter.

Chauncey (Middle English) chancellor; church official. *Chance*

Chavivi (Hebrew) beloved. *Chaviv, Habib*

Chen (Chinese) vast; great.

Chester (Old English) from the fortified camp. Short form of Rochester. *Ches, Cheston, Chet*

Chet short form of Chester.

Cheung (Chinese) good luck.

Chi (African) personal guardian angel.

Chic, Chick common forms of Charles. *Chickle, Chicky*

Chico (Spanish) common form of Francis (from Francisco).

Chilton (Old English) from the farm by the spring. *Chil, Chilt*

Chris short form of Christian; Christopher.

Christian (Greek) follower of Christ. *Chris, Krispin, Kristlan*

Christopher (Greek) Christ-bearer. Honoring St. Christopher. *Chris, Cristobal, Christos, Kit*

Chuck common form of Charles.

Chung (Chinese) intelligent.

Chung-Ae (Korean) righteous love.

Cid (Spanish) a lord. 11th-century Spanish hero. *Cyd, Sid*

Ciqala (American Indian) little.

Clarence (Latin) bright; famous. *Clarance, Clare*

Clark (Old French) scholar. *Clarke, Clerk*

Claude (Latin) lame. *Claudell, Claudio, Claus*

Clay (Old English) from the earth. Short form of Clayborne; Clayton.

Clayborne (Old English) born of the earth. *Claiborn, Clay*

Clayton (Old English) from the farm built on clay. *Clay*

Clement (Latin) merciful. *Clem, Clemens, Clemente*

Cleveland (Old English) from the cliffs. *Cleve, Clevey*

Cliff (Old English) steep rock, cliff. Short form of Clifford.

Clifford (Old English) from the cliff at the river crossing. *Cliff*

Clifton (Old English) from the town near the cliffs. *Clift*

Clint short form of Clinton.

Clinton (Old English) from the headland farm. *Clint*

Clive (Old English) from the cliff. *Cliff, Clyve*

Clyde (Scottish Gaelic) rocky eminence; heard from afar; (Welsh) warm. *Cly*

Cody (Old English) a cushion. Honoring Buffalo Bill Cody. *Codi*

Colbert (Old English) outstanding seafarer. *Cole, Colt, Culbert*

Colby (Old English) from the black farm. *Cole*

Coleman (Old English) adherent of Nicholas. *Cole, Colman*

Colin (Irish Gaelic) child. Common form of Nicholas. *Colan, Collin*

Collier (Old English) miner.

Colton (Old English) from the coal town. *Colt*

Coman (Arabic) noble.

Conan (Old English) intelligent. *Con, Conant, Conn, Conney*

Conlan (Irish Gaelic) hero. *Conlen, Conley, Conlin*

Connor (Irish Gaelic) wise aid.

Conrad (Old German) honest counselor. *Conn, Conrade, Kurt*

Conroy (Irish Gaelic) wise man. *Con, Roy*

Constantine (Latin) firm; constant. *Con, Conn, Conney, Connie, Conny, Constantin, Constantino, Costa, Konstantin, Konstantine*

Conway (Irish Gaelic) hound of the plain. *Conn, Conney*

Coujoe (African) born on Monday.

Cornell (French) form of Cornelius. *Corney, Cory*

Cort (Old German) bold; (Scandinavian) short. *Courtney, Curtis, Kort*

Cory short form of names beginning with Cor.

Cooper (Old English) barrelmaker. *Coop*

Corbett (Latin) raven. *Corbet, Corbin, Corby, Cory*

Cordell (Old French) ropemaker. *Cord, Cordy, Cory*

Corey (Irish Gaelic) from the hollow. *Cori, Cory, Kory*

Cornelius (Latin) horn-colored. *Cornell, Corney, Neel*

Courtland (Old English) from the farmstead or court land. *Court*

Courtney (Old French) from the court. *Cort, Curtis*

Cowan (Irish Gaelic) hillside hollow. *Coe, Cowey*

Craig (Irish Gaelic) from near the crag. *Craggie, Craggy*

Crandall (Old English) from the cranes' valley. *Cran, Crandell*

Crawford (Old English) from the ford of the crow. *Craw, Ford*

Creighton (Old English) from the estate near the creek. *Creigh, Creight, Crichton*

Crispin (Latin) curly haired.

Cromwell (Old English) dweller by the winding brook.

Crosby (Scandinavian) Persian emperor from the shrine of the cross. *Cross*

Cullen (Irish Gaelic) handsome. *Cull, Cullan, Culley*

Culver (Old English) dove. *Colver, Cull, Cully*

Curran (Irish Gaelic) hero. *Curr, Currey, Curry*

Curtis (Latin) short. *Curt, Curtice, Kurtis*

Cutler (Old English) knifemaker. *Cutty*

Cy short form of Cyril; Cyrus.

Cyril (Greek) lordly. *Cy, Cyrill,*

Cyrus (Persian) sun.

D

Dabir (Arabic) secretary, teacher.

Da-chun (Chinese) long spring.

Dada (African) child with curly hair.

Dag (Scandinavian) day or brightness. *Dagny*

Dagan (Hebrew) corn, grain.

Dahab (Arabic) gold.

Dale (Old English) from the valley. *Dal*

Dallas (Irish Gaelic) wise. *Dallis*

Dalton (Old English) from the estate in the valley. *Dal, Dalt, Tony*

Damek (Slavic) man of the earth. Form of Adam. *Adham, Damick*

Damian (German) form of Damon.

Damon (Greek) constant; tamer. *Dame, Damian, Damien*

Dan (Vietnamese) yes; short form of Daniel.

Dana (Scandinavian) Dane.

Dane (Old English) from Denmark. *Danie*

Daniel (Hebrew) God is my Judge. *Dan, Dani, Danny*

Dante (Latin) lasting.

Darby (Irish Gaelic) free man; (Old Norse) from the deer estate. *Dar, Darb, Derby*

Darcy (Irish Gaelic) dark. *Dar, Darce*

Daren (African) born at night. *Dare*

Darius (Greek) wealthy. *Dario, Derry*

Darnell (Old English) from the hidden place. *Dar, Darn, Darnall*

Darrel (French) beloved. *Dare, Darrill, Darryl*

Darren (Irish Gaelic) great. Common form of Dorian. *Daren, Darin*

Darwin (Old English) beloved friend. *Derwin*

Daudi (African) beloved one. *Daudy*

Dave short form of David; Davis. *Davie, Davy*

David (Hebrew) beloved. First King of Israel. *Dave, Davidson, Davon*

Davis (Old English) son of David. *Dave, Davie, Davy*

Dawid (Arabic) beloved.

Dean (Old English) from the valley. *Dino*

Dedrick (Old German) ruler of people. *Dedric*

Delaney (Irish Gaelic) descendant of the challenger. *Delainey*

Delano (Old French) of the night.

Delbert (Old English) bright as day.

Delmore (Old French) from the sea. *Del, Delmar*

Delsin (American Indian) he is so.

Delwin (Old English) proud friend. *Del, Delwyn*

Dembe (African) peace.

Demetrius (Greek) belonging to Demeter (goddess of fertility).

Dempsey (Irish Gaelic) proud. *Demp*

Denby (Scandinavian) from the village of the Danes. *Danby, Denny*

Dennis (Greek) of Dionysus, god of wine. *Denis, Dennison, Dion*

Dennison (Old English) son of Dennis. *Den, Denison*

Denny short form of names beginning with Den. *Den, Denney, Dennie*

Denton (Old English) from the valley estate. *Den, Dent, Denten*

Deon (French) god. *Dion, Dione*

Derek (Old German) ruler of the people. Short form of Theodoric. *Darrick, Derick, Dirk*

Dermot (Irish Gaelic) free from envy. *Der, Dermott, Diarmid*

Deron (Hebrew) bird; freedom.

Derry (Irish Gaelic) redhaired.

Déshì (Chinese) man of virtue.

Desmond (Irish Gaelic) man from south Munster. *Des, Desi, Desmund*

Devin (Irish Gaelic) poet. *Dev, Devy*

Devlin (Irish Gaelic) brave; fierce. *Dev, Devland, Devlen*

DeWitt (Flemish) blond. *Dwight, Wit*

Dexter (Latin) dexterous. *Deck, Dex*

Dick short form of Richard. *Dickie, Dicky*

Diego (Spanish) form of James.

Dietrich (German) form of Theodoric.

Dillon (Irish Gaelic) faithful. *Dill, Dillie, Dilly, Dylan*

Dimitri (Greek) belonging to Demeter, Greek god of fertility; (Russian) form of Demetrius.

Din (Vietnamese) settle down.

Dion (Greek) form of Dionysos.

Dirk short form of Derek; Theodoric.

Dolf, Dolph short forms of Adolph.

Dominic (Latin) belonging to the Lord. *Dom, Domenico, Domingo*

Don short form of names beginning with Don. *Donnie*

Donahue (Irish Gaelic) dark warrior. *Don, Donny, Donohue*

Donald (Irish Gaelic) world ruler. *Don, Donall, Donaugh, Donnie*

Dong-Sun (Korean) goodness of East. *Dong-Yul*

Donnelly (Irish Gaelic) brave dark man. *Donnell, Donnie, Donny*

Donovan (Irish Gaelic) dark warrior. *Don, Donavon*

Dorian (Greek) from the sea. *Darren, Dory, Isidore*

Doron (Hebrew, Greek) gift. *Doran, Dorian, Dorran*

Doug short form of Douglas. *Dougie, Dougy*

Douglas (Scottish Gaelic) from the dark water. *Doug, Douglass, Dugaid*

Dov (Hebrew) bear. Short form of David.

Doyle (Irish Gaelic) dark stranger. *Doy*

Drew (Old French) sturdy; (Old Welsh) wise. Short form of Andrew. *Dru, Drud*

Dryden (Old English) from the dry valley. *Dry*

Duane (Irish Gaelic) little and dark. *Dwain, Dwayne*

Duc (Vietnamese) moral. *Duy*

Dudley (Old English) from the people's meadow. *Dud*

Duff (Celtic) dark. *Duffy*

Duke (Old French) leader; duke. *Dukey, Duky*

Duncan (Scottish Gaelic) dark-skinned warrior. *Dunc, Dunn*

Dunham (Celtic) dark man.

Durant (Latin) enduring. *Dante, Durand, Durante*

Durojaiye (African) wait and enjoy what the world offers.

Durward (Old English) gatekeeper; doorward. *Derward, Ward*

Dustin (Old German) valiant fighter. *Dust, Dustan, Duston, Dusty*

Dwayne form of Duane.

Dwight (Modern English) form of De Witt.

Dyami (American Indian) an eagle.

Dylan (Old Welsh) from the sea. *Dillon, Dilan*

E

Eamon (Irish) wealthy guardian; fortunate warrior. Form of Edmund.

Earl (Old English) nobleman. *Earle, Erle, Errol*

Eaton (Old English) from the estate on the river. *Eatton*

Ebbo (African) born on Tuesday.

Enen (Hebrew) rock. *Eben, Ebeneser, Ebenezer*

Ed short form of names beginning with Ed. *Edan, Eddie, Eddy*

Eden (Hebrew) delight. *Ed*

Edgar (Old English) successful spearman. *Ed, Edgard, Edgardo, Ned, Teddie*

Edison (Old English) son of Edward. *Ed, Eddy, Edson*

Edmund (Old English) prosperous protector. *Eamon, Eddie, Edmon,Teddie*

Edsel (Old English) from the rich man's house. *Ed, Eddie, Eddy*

Edward (Old English) happy guardian. *Ed, Eddie, Eddy*

Edwin (Old English) rich friend. *Eddy, Ned, Teddy*

Efia (African) born on Friday.

Efrayim (Hebrew) fruitful. *Efrem, Ephraim, Ephrem*

Efrem (Hebrew) modern form of Ephraim.

Egan (Irish Gaelic) ardent, fiery. *Egon*

Egbert (Old English) bright as a sword. *Bert, Bertie*

Eginhard (German) sword strength. *Einhard, Egon, Enno*

Egon (Scandinavian) formidable.

Ehud (Hebrew) biblical name.

Ejau (African) we have received.

Ekundayo (African) sorrow becomes happiness.

Elden, Eldon forms of Alden. *Elton*

Eldred (Old English) sage counsel. *Aldred, Eldrid*

Eldridge form of Aldrich. *El, Eldredge*

Eli (Hawaiian) Jehovah the highest; (Hebrew) height. Short form of Eleazar; Elijah; Elisha. *Ely*

Elias (Greek) form of Elijah; (American Indian) Jehovah is God.

Elisha (Hebrew) God is salvation. *Eli, Ely*

Eleizar (Hebrew) God has helped. *Eli, Elie, Eliezer, Ely*

Eleutherious (Greek) freedom.

Elijah (Hebrew) Jehovah is God. *Elias, Eliot, Ellis*

Elika (Hawaiian) ever powerful.

Elisha (Hebrew) the Lord is salvation. *Eli, Eliseo, Elish, Ely*

Ellery (Old English) elder tree. *Ellary, Ellerey*

Elliott (Hebrew) close to God. Modern English form of Elijah. *Eliot, Eliott, Elliot*

Ellis (Hebrew) modern form of Elijah (from Elias).

Ellison (Old English) son of Elias. *Elson*

Ellsworth (Old English) nobleman's estate. *Ellswerth, Elsworth*

Elmer (Old English) famous.

Elmo (Italian) helmet; protector. Common form of Anselm. *Elmore*

Elroy form of Leroy.

Elton (Old English) from the old town. *Alden, Aldon, Eldon*

Elvis (Scandinavian) all wise. Form of Elwin. *Al, Alvis*

Elwood (Old English) from the old wood. *Ellwood, Woody*

Emerson (Old German/English) son of the industrious ruler.

Emery (Old German) industrious ruler. *Amory, Emory*

Emil (Latin) flattering; winning. *Emile, Emilio*

Enapay (American Indian) comes out.

Engelbert (Old German) bright as an angel. *Bert, Bertie, Berty, Englebert, Ingelbert, Inglebert*

Enoch (Hebrew) dedicated; consecrated.

Enos (Hebrew) man.

Enrico (Italian) form of Henry.

Enzo (Teutonic) ruler of an estate. From Henry.

Erasmus (Greek) lovable. *Erasme, Erasmo*

Erastus (Greek) beloved. *Ras, Rastus*

Erhard (Old German) strong resolution. *Erhart*

Eric (Scandinavian) ever-ruler; ever-powerful. Short form of Frederick. *Erik, Rick, Ricky*

Erhardt (Old German) honor.

Erin (Irish Gaelic) peace.

Ernest (Old English) earnest. *Ernesto, Ernst*

Erno (Old German) serious.

Errol (German) form of Earl. *Erroll, Rollo*

Erskine (Scottish Gaelic) from the height of the cliff. *Kin, Kinny*

Ervin, Erwin forms of Irving.

Ethan (Hebrew) firm.

Etiénne (French/Greek) crowned with laurels.

Etu (American Indian) the sun.

Eugene (Greek) well-born. *Eugéne, Eugenio, Gene*

Eustace (Greek) steadfast; (Latin) rich in corn. *Eustache, Eustasius, Eustazio, Eustis, Stacie, Stacy*

Evan (Welsh) young warrior; form of John. *Evin, Owen*

Everhard (Old English) strong as a bear.

Everett (Old English) strong as a boar. *Eberhard, Everard, Evered, Ewart*

Ewansiha (African) secrets are not for sale.

Ezekiel (Hebrew) strength of God. *Zeke*

Ezer (Hebrew) help, helper. *Azrikam, Azur, Ezra, Ezri.*

Ezhno (American Indian) solitary; a loner.

F

Fabian (Latin) bean grower. *Fabiano, Fabio*

Fabrice (French) craftsman.

Fadil (Arabic) generous.

Fahd (Arabic) lynx.

Fairfax (Old English) fairhaired. *Fax*

Fakhir (Arabic) proud; excellent.

Falkner (Old English) trainer of falcons. *Faulkner, Fowler*

Farley (Old English) from the bull or sheep meadow. *Fairleigh*

Farrell (Irish Gaelic) heroic.

Favian (Latin) a man of understanding.

Faysal (Arabic) decisive.

Feivel (Hebrew) God aids.

Felix (Latin) fortunate. *Felic*

Felton (Old English) from the estate built on the meadow. *Felt, Felten*

Fenton (Old English) from the marshland farm. *Fen*

Ferdinand (Old German) adventurous; brave. *Ferd, Ferdie, Fergus, Hernando*

Fidel (Latin) faithful. *Fidele, Fidelio*

Fielding (Old English) from the field. *Field*

Filbert (Old English) brilliant. *Bert, Filberto, Phil, Philbert*

Filmore (Old English) very famous. *Filmer, Phil*

Finlay (Irish Gaelic) little fair-haired soldier. *Fin, Finley*

Finn (Scandinavian) he who finds. Short form of Finlay. *Finnie, Finny*

Fitzgerald (Old English) mighty with a spear. *Fitz, Gerry*

Fitzpatrick (Old English) son of a nobleman. *Pat, Patrick*

Flavian (Latin) blonde, yellow-haired. *Flavio, Flavius*

Fleming (Old English) Dutchman. *Flem, Flemming*

Fletcher (Old French) arrow-featherer. *Fletch*

Flint (Old English) stream.

Florian (Latin) flowering, blooming. *Flory*

Floyd (English) form of Lloyd.

Flynn (Irish Gaelic) son of the red-haired man. *Flin, Flinn*

Folke (German) people's guard. *Volker*

Foluke (American Indian) placed in God's hand.

Foma (Russian) twin.

Forbes (Irish Gaelic) prosperous.

Ford (Old English) river crossing. Short form of names ending in -ford.

Forest, Forrest (Old French) forest; woodsman. *Forester, Forster, Foster*

Fortune (Old French) lucky. *Fortunato*

Foster (Latin) keeper of the woods. Form of Forrest.

Fowler (Old English) trapper of wild fowl. *Falconer, Falkner*

Francis (Latin) Frenchman. *Francesco, Frank, Franz, Paco, Pancho*

Francois (French) form of Francis.

Frank short form of
Francis; Franklin.
Frankie, Franky

Franklin (Middle
English) free landowner.
Fran, Frank, Franklyn

Franz (German) free.

Frazer (Old English)
curly-haired; (Old French)
strawberry. *Fraser, Frasier*

Fred short form of names
containing Fred. *Freddie,
Freddy*

Frederic (Old German)
peaceful ruler. *Eric,
Federico, Fred, Freddie,
Frederico, Rick*

Freeman (Old English)
free man. *Free,
Freedman, Freeland,
Freemon*

Fremont (Old German)
guardian of freedom.
Free, Monty

Frik (German) common
form of Frederick.

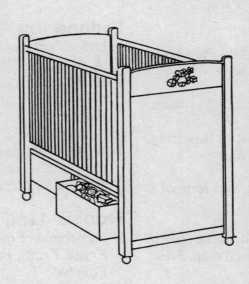

G

Gabriel (Hebrew) devoted to God. *Gabby, Gabe, Gabriele*

Gage (Old French) pledge.

Galabba (African) talking.

Gale (Irish Gaelic) stranger; (Old English) gay, lively. Short form of Galen. *Gayle*

Galen (Irish Gaelic) intelligent. *Gaelan, Gale*

Gallagher (Irish Gaelic) eager helper.

Galvin (Irish Gaelic) sparrow.

Gannon (Irish Gaelic) fair-complected.

Gardner (Middle English) gardener. *Gar*

Gareth (Welsh) gentle. *Gar, Garth*

Garfield (Old English) battlefield.

Garland (Old English) from the battlefield; (Old French) wreath. *Gar, Garlen*

Garner (Old French) armed sentry. *Gar*

Garnett (Old English) armed with a spear; (Latin) pomegranate seed; stone. *Gar*

Gan (Chinese) dare; adventure; (Vietnamese) to be near.

Garrett (Old English) with a mighty spear. *Garth, Garrard, Garreth, Jarret*

Garrick (Old English) oak spear. *Garik, Garrek*

Garth (Scandinavian) grounds keeper. *Garrett.*

Garvey (Irish Gaelic) rough peace.

Garvin (Old English) comrade in battle. *Garwin, Vinnie*

Gary (Old English) spear carrier. Common form of Gerald. *Garry*

Gaston (French) man from Gascony.

Gavi (Hebrew) God is my strength. *Gabriel*.

Gavin (Welsh) white hawk. *Gavan, Gawain*

Gaylord (Old French) gay lord; jailer. *Gallard, Gay, Gayelord, Gayler, Gaylor*

Gaynor (Irish Gaelic) son of the fair-complected man. *Gainer, Gainor*

Gene common form of Eugene.

Geno (Italian) form of John. *Jeno*

Geoffrey (English) form of Godfrey; Jeffrey. *Geoff, Jeff*

George (Greek) farmer. *Giorgio, Goran, Jorgan, Yurik*

Gerald (Old German) warrior, spear ruler. *Gary, Gerard, Gerick, Giraud, Jerald*

Gerard (Old English) warrior, spear ruler. *Gerardo, Géraud, Gerhard, Gerhardt, Gerrard, Gerri, Gerrie, Gerry, Gherardo*

Germain (Middle English) sprout, bud. *Germaine, Germayne, Jermain, Jermaine, Jermayne*

Gershom (Hebrew) exile. *Gersham*

Ghalib (Arabic) victor.

Gia (Vietnamese) family.

Giacomo (Italian) form of Jacob. *Giacamo, Gian*

Gideon (Hebrew) feller of trees; destroyer.

Gifford (Old English) bold giver. *Giff*

Gilad (Arabic) camel hump. *Giladi, Gilead*.

Gilbert (Old English)
trusted. *Bert, Bertie, Burt,
Gibb, Gil, Gilberto,
Wilbert, Wilbur, Will*

Gilchrist (Irish Gaelic)
servant of Christ. *Gil,
Gillie*

Giles (Greek) shield
bearer. *Gil, Gill, Gilles*

Gilmore (Irish Gaelic)
devoted to the Virgin
Mary. *Gil, Gill, Gillmore,
Gilmour*

Gilroy (Irish Gaelic)
devoted to the king. *Gil,
Gill, Gillie, Roy*

Gino (Italian) short form
of Ambrose; Louis.

Giovanni (Italian) form
of John. *Gian, Gianni*

Giuseppe (Italian) form
of Joseph.

Gladwin (Old English)
cheerful. *Glad, Win,
Winnie, Winny*

Glen, Glenn (Irish
Gaelic) valley. Short form
of Glendon. *Glyn, Glynn*

Glendon (Scottish
Gaelic) from the glen
fortress. *Glen, Glenn*

Godfrey (German) form
of Jeffrey (from
Gottfried). *Geoff,
Geoffrey, Godfry*

Godwin (Old English)
friend of God. *Goodwin,
Win, Winnie, Winny*

Gomda (American
Indian) wind.

Gonza (African) love.

Gordon (Old English)
hill of the plains. *Gordan,
Gorden, Gordie, Gordy*

Gowon (African)
rainmaker.

Grady (Irish Gaelic)
noble; illustrious.

Graham (Latin) a grain.
(English) the gray home.

Granger (Old English)
farmer. *Grange, Gray*

Grant (French) great.
Short form of Grantland.
*Grantham, Grantley,
Grenville*

Grantland (Old English) from the great plains. *Grant*

Granville (Old French) from the large town. *Gran, Grannie, Granny*

Grayson (Old English) son of a bailiff. *Gray, Grey, Greyson, Son, Sonny*

Greg short form of Gregory. *Graig, Gregg*

Gregor (Scottish) form of Gregory.

Gregory (Latin) watchman; watchful. *Graig, Greg, Gregg, Greggory*

Griffin (Latin) griffin (a mythical beast). *Griff, Griffie, Griffith, Griffy*

Griffith (Welsh) fierce chief; ruddy. *Griffin, Griff, Griffie, Griffy*

Griswold (Old German) from the gray forest. *Gris, Griz*

Grover (Old English) from the grove. *Grove*

Guido (German/Italian/Spanish/Swedish) form of Guy.

Guillermo (Spanish) form of William.

Gunther (Scandinavian) battle army; warrior. *Gun, Gunnar, Gunner, Guntar, Gunter*

Gurion (Hebrew) young lion.

Gurpreet (Indian) devoted to the prophet.

Gus (Greek) nickname for Constantinos.

Gustave (Scandinavian) staff of the Goths. *Gus, Gustaf, Gustav, Gustavus*

Guthrie (Irish Gaelic) from the windy place; (Old German) war hero. *Guthrey, Guthry*

Guy (French) guide; (Hebrew) valley; (Old German) warrior. *Guido*

Guyapi (American Indian) candid.

Gyasi (African) wonderful child.

H

Hadley (Old English) from the heath. *Hadlee, Hadleigh, Lee, Leigh*

Haji (African) born during month of pilgrimage to Mecca.

Hakan (American Indian) fiery.

Hakim (Arabic) wise. *Hakeem*

Hakon (Scandinavian) of the chosen race.

Hakulani (Hawaiian) star in heaven.

Hal short form of Harold; Henry; names beginning with Hal.

Haldan (Scandinavian) half-Danish. *Dan, Dannie, Danny, Don, Donnie, Donny, Hal, Halden*

Haley (Irish Gaelic) ingenious. *Hailey, Haily, Hal, Hale, Lee, Leigh*

Hall (Old English) from the manor or hall.

Halsey (Old English) from Hal's island. *Hal, Hallsy, Halsy*

Halstead (Old English) from the manor. *Hal, Halsted, Steady*

Hamal (Arabic) lamb.

Hamid (Arabic) thanking God.

Hamidi (African) commendable.

Hamilton (Old English) from the proud estate. *Ham, Hamel, Hamil, Tony*

Hamlet (Old French/German) little home. *Ham*

Hamlin (Old French/German) little home-lover. *Ham, Hamlen, Lin, Lynn*

Hanale (Teutonic/ Hawaiian) ruler of an estate. *Haneke*

Hank common form of Henry.

Hans (Scandinavian) form of John.

Harcourt (Old French) fortified dwelling. *Court, Harry*

Hardy (Old German) bold and daring.

Harley (Old English) from the long field; from the army meadow.

Harlow (Old English) from the rough hill or army hill. *Arlo*

Harmon (English) form of Herman.

Harold (Scandinavian) army ruler. *Hal, Harald, Harry, Herold, Herrick*

Harper (Old English) harp player.

Harrison (Old English) son of Harry. *Harris*

Harry (Old English) soldier. Short form of Harold; Henry. *Harrison.*

Hart (Old English) hart (male) deer. Short form of Hartley. *Harwill*

Hartley (Old English) from the deer meadow. *Hart*

Harvey (Old German) army warrior. *Harv, Herve, Hervey*

Hasam (Arabic) beautiful.

Hashim (Arabic) destroyer of evil. *Hasheem*

Hasani (African) handsome. *Husani*

Hasin (Indian) laughing. *Hasen, Hassin*

Haskel (Hebrew) understanding. *Haskell*

Haslett (Old English) from the hazel tree land. *Haze, Hazel, Hazlett*

Hasan (Arabic) beautiful.

Hastings (Old English) son of the stern man. *Hasty*

Havelock (Scandinavian) sea battle.

Hayden (Old English) from the hedged valley.

Hayes (Old English) from the hedged place.

Hayward (Old English) guardian of the hedged area.

Haywood (Old English) from the hedged forest. *Heywood, Woodie, Woody*

Hea (Korean) grace.

Heath (Middle English) from the heath.

Hector (Greek) steadfast.

Henderson (Old English/Scottish) son of Henry.

Henri (French) form of Henry.

Henry (Old German) ruler of an estate. *Enrico, Enrique, Hal, Hank, Harry, Heinrich, Hendrick, Henri*

Herbert (Old German) glorious soldier. *Bert, Bertie, Berty, Herb, Herbie, Herby*

Hercules (Greek) glorious gift. *Hercule*

Herman (Latin) high-ranking person; (Old German) warrior. *Armand, Armando, Harman, Harmon, Hermann, Hermie, Hermon*

Hernando (Spanish) form of Ferdinand.

Hershel (Hebrew) deer. *Hersch, Herschel, Hersh, Hirsch*

Hiamovi (American Indian) high chief.

Hideaki (Japanese) wisdom; clever person.

Hilary (Latin) cheerful.

Hillard (Old German) brave warrior.

Hillel (Hebrew) greatly praised.

Hilliard (Old German) war guardian. *Hillard*

Hiroshi (Japanese) generous.

Hilton (Old English) from the town on the hill.

Hiram (Hebrew) most noble. *Hi, Hy*

Ho (Chinese) the good.

Hobart (Old German) bright mind.

Hod (Hebrew) vigorous; splendid.

Hogan (Irish Gaelic) youth.

Holbrook (Old English) from the brook in the hollow. *Brook, Holbrooke*

Holden (Old English) from the hollow in the valley.

Hollis (Old English) from the grove of holly trees.

Holmes (Middle English) from the river islands.

Holt (Old English) from the forest.

Homer (Greek) promise.

Hop (Chinese) agreeable.

Horace (Latin) keeper of the hours.

Horst (Old German) a thicket.

Horton (Old English) from the gray estate.

Hoshea (Hebrew) salvation. *Hosea, Hosheah*

Houston (Old English) hill town.

Howard (Old English) watchman. *Howey, Ward*

Hubert (Old German) bright mind. *Bert, Hobard, Hobart, Huey, Hugh*

Hugh (Old English) intelligence. Short form of Hubert. *Huey, Hugo*

Hulbert (Old German) brilliant grace. *Bert, Bertie, Berty, Burt, Hulbard, Hulburt, Hull*

Humbert (Old German) brilliant Hun. *Hum, Umberto*

Humphrey (Old German) peaceful Hun. *Humfried, Hump, Onofredo*

Hung (Chinese) great.

Hunt (Old English) hunt. Short form of names beginning with Hunt.

Hunter (Old English) hunter. *Hunt*

Huntington (Old English) hunting estate. *Hunt, Huntingdon*

Huntley (Old English) hunter's meadow. *Hunt, Huntlee, Lee*

Husam (Arabic) sword.

Hutton (Old English) from the house on the jutting ledge. *Huttan*

Huxley (Old English) from Hugh's meadow. *Hux, Lee, Leigh*

Hyatt (Old English) from the high gate. *Hy*

Hy (Vietnamese) hope.

Hyo (Korean) filial duty.

Hyun (Korean) wisdom.

Hywel (Welsh) eminent.

I

Ian form of John.

Iban (Basque) God's gracious gift. *Jon*

Ibon (Teutonic) archer.

Ibrahim (Arabic) my father is exalted.

Idris (Arabic) name of a prophet.

Igor (Russian) form of Inger.

Illan (Latin/Basque) youth.

Imad (Arabic) support, pillar.

Imarogbe (African) child born to a good family.

Imre (Teutonic) industrious.

Ince (Latin) innocent.

Inder (Hindi) name of a god.

Ingemar (Scandinavian) famous son. *Ingmar*

Inger (Scandinavian) son's army. *Igor, Ingar*

Inglebert form of Engelbert.

Ingram (Old English) angel.

Innis (Celtic) from the island. *Inness*

Ioan (Hebrew) God's gracious gift. *Ivan*

Ioannes (Greek) God's gracious gift. *Giannes, Ioannikios, Jannes, Yanni, John*

Iokepa (Hawaiian) God will add. Form of Joseph.

Ira (Hebrew) watchful.

Irving (Irish Gaelic) beautiful; (Old English) sea friend. *Ervin, Erwin, Irvin, Irvine, Irwin*

Isaac (Hebrew) laughter. *Ike, Isaak, Isac, Izak*

Isas (Japanese) meritorious.

Isidore (Greek) gift of Isis. *Dore, Dory, Izzy*

Iskander (Greek) defender of mankind.

Israel (Hebrew) ruling with the Lord; wrestling with the Lord.

Issa (African) God is our salvation.

Isser (Hebrew) Israel.

Ivan (Russian) form of John.

Ivar (Teutonic/ Scandinavian) archer. *Ive, Iver, Ivor*

Ixidor (Greek) a gift of ideas.

Iyapo (African) many trials.

Iye (American Indian) smoke.

J

Jabir (Arabic) consoler, comforter.

Jabari (African) brave.

Jacinto (Spanish/Greek) purple flower.

Jack common form of Jacob; John. Short form of Jackson. *Jock, Jocko*

Jackson (Old English) son of Jack. *Jack*

Jacob (Hebrew) supplanter. *Cob, Jack, Jacobo, Jacques, Jamie, Shamus*

Jacques (French) form of Jacob; James.

Jacy (American Indian) the moon; creator of all plant life.

Jael (Hebrew) to ascend. *Yael*

Jaime (Spanish) form of James.

Jake short form of Jacob.

Jamal (Arabic) beauty. Form of Gamal. *Jamaal, Jamil, Jammal*

James (English) held by the heel; supplanter. Form of Jacob. *Jaime, Jim, Jimmy, Seamus*.

Jamil (Arabic) handsome.

Jareb (Hebrew) he will contend. *Jarib*

Jared (Hebrew) one who rules. *Jarad, Jarred, Jarrod*

Jarrett form of Garrett

Jarvis (Old German) sharp spear. *Jervis*

Jason (Greek) healer. *Jay, Jayson*

Jasper (English) precious stone. Form of Casper.

Jay (Old French) blue jay. Common form of Jacob; James; Jason.

Jean (French) form of John.

Jed (Hebrew) beloved of the Lord. Short form of Jedidiah.

Jeff short form of Jefferson; Jeffrey. Common form of Geoffrey.

Jefferson (Old English) son of Jeffrey. *Jeff*

Jeffrey (Old French) heavenly peace. *Geoffrey, Gottfried, Jefferey*

Jeremiah (Hebrew) appointed by Jehovah. *Jeremias, Jeremy, Jerry*

Jeremy modern form of Jeremiah. *Jeramey, Jeremie, Jeromy*

Jerome (Latin) holy name.

Jerry short form of Gerald; Jeremiah; Jeremy; Jerome.

Jesse (Hebrew) God exists. *Jessie*

Jesus (Hebrew) God will help.

Jethro (Hebrew) pre-eminence. *Jeth*

Jim short form of James. *Jimmie, Jimmy*

Jimiyu (African) born in a dry season.

Jin (Chinese) gold.

Jiro (Japanese) the second.

Job (Hebrew) the afflicted.

Jock common form of Jacob; John. *Jocko*

Joe short form of Joseph. *Joey*

Joel (Hebrew) Jehovah is the Lord.

John (Hebrew) God is gracious. *Evan, Jack, Jan, Owen, Sean, Zane*

Jojo (African) born on Monday.

Jon form of John. Short form of Jonathan.

Jonah (Hebrew) dove. *Jonas*

Jonas (Hebrew) the doer.

Jonathan (Hebrew) Jehovah gave. *Jonathon*

Jordan (Hebrew) descending. *Jared, Jordon, Jory*

Jose (Spanish) form of Joseph. *Pepe, Pepito*

Joseph (Hebrew) he shall add.

Josh short form of Joshua.

Joshua (Hebrew) Jehovah saves. *Josh, Joshia*

Juan (Spanish) form of John.

Judah (Hebrew) praised. *Jud, Judas, Judd, Jude*

Jude (Latin) right in the law.

Jules (French) form of Julius. *Jule*

Julian (Latin) belonging or related to Julius.

Julius (Greek) youthful. *Jule, Jules, Julian, Julie, Julio*

Juma (African) born on Friday.

Jumoke (African) everyone loves this child.

Jun (Chinese) truth; (Japanese) obedient; purity.

Justin (Latin) upright. *Justen, Justinian, Justino*

Juvénal (French/Latin) youth.

K

Kadar (Arabic) powerful.
Kedar

Kadri (Arabic) my destiny.

Kaipo (Hawaiian) the sweetheart.

Kalil (Arabic) good friend.
Kahlil

Kamaka (Hawaiian) the face.

Kane (Japanese) one's own kind.

Kareem (Arabic) noble, exalted.

Karl (German) form of Charles. *Kale, Kalle, Karlan, Karlens, Karlik, Karlis*

Kato (African) second of the twins to be born.

Kayode (African) he brought joy.

Kazuo (Japanese) man of peace.

Keane (Old English) sharp, keen. *Kean, Keen, Keenan, Keene*

Keenan (Irish Gaelic) little and ancient. *Keen*

Keir (Celtic) dark-skinned. *Kerr.*

Keith (Welsh) from the forest; (Scottish Gaelic) from the battle place.

Kekoa (Hawaiian) courageous one.

Kelly (Irish Gaelic) warrior. *Kelley*

Kelsey (Scandinavian) from the ship-island.

Ken short form of names containing -ken-. *Kenn, Kennie, Kenny*

Kendall (Old English) from the bright valley. *Ken, Kendell, Kennie, Kenny*

Kennedy (Irish Gaelic) helmeted chief. *Ken, Kenn, Kenny*

Kenneth (Irish Gaelic) handsome; (Old English) royal oath. *Ken, Kenn, Kennet, Kennett, Kenny*

Kent (Welsh) white, bright. Short form of Kenton. *Ken, Kenn, Kenny*

Kenton (Old English) from the king's estate. *Ken, Kenn, Kenny, Kent*

Kenyon (Irish Gaelic) white-haired, blond. *Ken, Kenn, Kenny*

Keola (Hawaiian) the life.

Kerman (Basque) strength.

Kermit (Irish Gaelic) free man. *Kermie, Kermy, Kerr*

Kerr (Scandinavian) marshland.

Kerry (Irish Gaelic) dark; dark-haired. *Keary*

Kesse (African) fat at birth.

Keung (Chinese) universe.

Kevin (Irish Gaelic) gentle, lovable. *Kev, Kevan, Keven, Kevon*

Khalil (Arabic) friend.

Kibbe (American Indian) the night bird.

Killian (Irish Gaelic) little and warlike. *Kilian, Killie, Killy*

Kim (Old English) chief, ruler. (Vietnamese) gold; metal.

Kimball (Old English) warrior chief; royal and bold. *Kim, Kimble*

Kincaid (Celtic) battle chief.

King (Old English) king.

Kingsley (Old English) from the king's meadow. *King, Kingsley, Kingsly, Kinsley*

Kingston (Old English) from the king's estate. *King*

Kipp (Old English) from the pointed hill. *Kip, Kippar, Kippie*

Kirk (Scandinavian) from the church. *Kerk*

Kit common form of Christian; Christopher.

Kiyoshi (Japanese) quiet.

Knox (Old English) from the hills.

Knud (Scandinavian) knot; kind.

Knute (Scandinavian) form of Canute.

Kono (American Indian) tree squirrel bites through pine nuts.

Kurt (German) form of Conrad.

Kwami (African) born on Saturday.

Kyle (Irish Gaelic) handsome; from the strait; (Hebrew) crowned with laurels. *Kiel, Kiley*

L

Laban (Hebrew) white.
Lavan

Labib (Arabic) sensible,
intelligent.

Ladd (Middle English)
attendant. *Lad, Laddie,
Laddy*

Laird (Scottish) landed
proprietor, laird.

Lamar (Old German)
famous throughout the
land. *Lemar*

Lambert (Old German)
bright land; bright as the
land. *Bert, Bertie, Berty*

Lamont (Scandinavian)
lawyer. *Monty*

Lance (Old German)
land. *Lancelot, Launce*

Landon (Old English)
from the open, grassy
meadow.

Lane (Middle English)
from the narrow road.
Laney, Lanie

Langdon (Old English)
from the long hill.

Langley (Old English)
from the long meadow.
Lang

Langston (Old English)
from the long, narrow
town. *Langsdon*

Lanny short form of
Orland; Roland. *Lannie,
Lennie*

Larry common form of
Lawrence.

Lars (Scandinavian) form
of Lawrence.

Lasse (Scandinavian/
Greek) victory of the
people.

Lateef (Arabic) gentle,
pleasant.

Lathrop (Old English)
from the barn-farmstead.

Laurent (Latin/French)
crowned with laurel.

Lavi (Hawaiian/Hebrew)
lion. *Lieb*

Lawford (Old English)
from the ford on the hill.
Ford, Law

Lawrence (Latin) from
Laurentium;
laurel-crowned. *Larry,
Lars, Lauren, Laurence,
Laurens, Laurent, Lon,
Lonnie, Lonny, Lorenzo,
Lorry, Rance*

Lawton (Old English)
from the estate on the hill.
Laughton, Law

Lazarus (Hebrew) God
will help.

Leander (Greek)
lionlike. *Leonard,
Leandro, Lee, Leigh, Leo*

Lee (Old English) from
the meadow. Short form
of names containing the
sound lee. *Leigh*

Leif (Scandinavian)
beloved. *Lief*

Leib (Hebrew) lion.

Leigh form of Lee.

Leighton (Old English)
from the meadow farm.
Layton

Leland (Old English)
meadowland. *Lee,
Leeland, Leigh*

Lemuel (Hebrew)
devoted to the Lord. *Lem,
Lemmie, Lemmy*

Len (American Indian)
flute.

Leo (Latin) lion. Short
form of Leander;
Leonard; Leopold. *Lee,
Leon, Lev, Lion, Lyon*

Leon (French) lion,
lion-like. Short form of
Leonard.

Leonard (Old German)
bold lion. *Leander, Lee,
Len, Lennie, Lenny, Leo,
Léon, Leonard, Leonardo,
Lonnie, Lonny*

Leopold (Old German)
bold for the people. *Leo*

Leroy (Old French) king. *Elroy, Lee, Leigh, LeRoy, Roy*

Les short form of Leslie; Lester.

Leslie (Scottish Gaelic) from the gray fortress. *Lee, Leigh, Les, Lesley*

Lester (Latin) from the chosen camp; (Old English) from Leicester. *Les*

Lev (Hebrew) heart. *Leb*

Levi (Hebrew) joined in harmony. *Levin, Levon, Levy*

Lewis short form of Llewellyn. Form of Louis. *Lew, Lewie*

Liam (Irish) form of William.

Liang (Chinese) good, excellent.

Lincoln (Old English) from the settlement by the pool. *Linc, Link*

Lindsay (Old English) from the linden tree island. *Lind, Lindsey*

Linus (Greek) flaxen-haired.

Lionel (Old French) lion cub.

Lloyd (Welsh) gray haired. *Floyd, Loy*

Locke (Old English) from the forest. *Lock, Lockwood*

Logan (Irish Gaelic) from the hollow.

Lon (Latin) lion. *Lonnie, Lonny*

London (Middle English) fortress of the moon.

Loren short form of Lawrence. *Lorin*

Lorimer (Latin) harness-maker. *Lorrie, Lorrimer, Lorry*

Lorne common form of Lawrence. *Lorn*

Louis (Old German) renowned warrior. *Aloysius, Lew, Lewis, Lou, Louie, Ludwig, Luigi, Luis*

Lowell (Old French) little wolf.

Lucian (Latin) shining, resplendent. *Luciano, Lucien*

Lucius (Latin) bringer of light. *Luca, Lucas, Luce, Lucian, Lukas, Luke*

Luckman (Arabic) prophet.

Ludlow (Old English) from the prince's hill; (English) from of Ludwig.

Ludwig (German) famous warrior. Form of Louis.

Luis (Spanish) form of Louis.

Luke (Greek) from Lucania. Form of Lucius. *Lucas, Lukas*

Lutalo (African) warrior.

Lyle (Old French) from the island. *Lisle, Lyell*

Lyndon (Old English) from the linden tree hiill. *Lin, Lindon, Lindy, Lyn, Lynn*

Lynn (Old English) waterfall; pool below a fall. *Lin, Linn, Lyn*

Lysander (Greek) liberator. *Sander*

M

Mac (Scottish Gaelic) son of. Short form of names beginning with Mac; Max; Mc. *Mack*

Mackenzie (Irish Gaelic) son of the wise leader. *Mac, Mack*

Madison (Old English) son of the powerful soldier. *Maddie, Maddy, Son, Sonnie, Sonny*

Magnus (Latin) great.

Mahmud (Arabic) praised.

Makya (American Indian) eagle hunter.

Malachi (Hebrew) angel; my messenger. *Mal, Malachy*

Malcolm (Scottish Gaelic) follower of St. Columba (an early Scottish saint). *Mal*

Malik (Arabic) master; king; angel.

Mallory (Old German) army counselor.

Malvin form of Melvin.

Mandel (German) almond. *Mannie, Manny*

Manchu (Chinese) pure.

Manfred (Old English) man of peace. *Fred, Freddie, Freddy, Mannie, Manny*

Manu (African) the second born. (Hawaiian) bird.

Manuel short form of Emmanuel. *Mano, Manolo*

Man-Young (Korean) ten thousand years of prosperity.

Marc (French) warlike. Form of Mark.

Marcel (Latin) little and warlike. *Marcello, Marcellus, Marcelo*

Marcus form of Mark.

Mario (Italian) form of Mark.

Marion (French) form of Mary usually reserved for boys.

Mark (Latin) warlike. *Marc, Marco, Marcos, Marcus, Markos*

Marlon (Old French) little falcon. Common form of Merlin. *Marlin*

Marlow (Old English) from the hill by the lake. *Marlo, Marlowe*

Marshall (Old French) steward; horse-keeper. *Marsh, Marshal*

Martin (Latin) warlike. *Marty*

Marty short form of Martin.

Marvin (Old English) lover of the sea. *Marv, Marve, Merwin, Merwyn*

Masahiro (Japanese) broad-minded.

Masao (Japanese) righteous.

Mason (Old French) stoneworker. *Mace, Sonnie, Sonny*

Matt short form of Matthew. *Mattie, Matty*

Matthew (Hebrew) gift of the Lord. *Mateo, Mathew, Mathias, Matt, Matthias, Mattie, Matty*

Mauli (Hawaiian) dark-skinned.

Maurice (Latin) dark-skinned. *Mauricio, Maurie, Maury, Moore, Morey, Morse, Morris*

Max short form of Maximilian; Maxwell. *Maxie, Maxy*

Maximilian (Latin) most excellent. *Mac, Mack, Max, Maxie, Maxim, Maxy*

Maxwell (Old English) from the influential man's well. *Mac, Mack, Max*

Mayer form of Major.

Mayir (Hebrew) enlightener. *Meir*

Maynard (Old German) powerful, brave.

Mbwana (African) master.

Mead (Old English) from the meadow. *Meade*

Melbourne (Old English) from the mill stream. *Mel, Melborn, Melburn*

Melville (Old English/Old French) from the estate of the hard worker. *Mel*

Melvin (Irish Gaelic) polished chief. *Mal, Malvin, Mel, Vin, Vinnle, Vinny*

Meredith (Welsh) guardian from the sea. *Merideth, Merry*

Merle (French) blackbird. Short form of Merlin; Merrill.

Merlin (Middle English) falcon. *Marlin, Marlon, Merle, Merrill*

Merrick (Old English) ruler of the sea.

Merrill (Old French) famous. *Merlin.*

Merton (Old English) from the town by the sea. *Merv, Merwyn*

Mervin form of Marvin. *Merwin, Merwyn*

Meyer (German) farmer; (Hebrew) bringer of light. *Major, Meier, Meir, Myer*

Micah (Hebrew) form of Michael. *Mic, Mick, Mike, Mikey, Myca Mycah*

Michael (Hebrew) who is like the Lord. *Micah, Michail, Michal, Michele, Mickey, Micky, Miguel, Mike, Mischa, Mitch, Mitchell*

Mike short form of Michael. *Mikey*

Miles (Latin) soldier; (Old German) merciful. *Milo, Myles*

Mililani (Hawaiian) heavenly caress.

Millard (Latin) caretaker of the mill. *Mill, Miller*

Milo (German) form of Miles.

Milton (Old English) from the mill town. *Milt, Miltie*

Mingan (American Indian) gray wolf.

Minkah (African) justice.

Mischa (Slavic) form of Michael.

Mitch short form of Mitchell.

Mitchell (Middle English) form of Michael. *Mitch, Mitchel*

Modupe (African) thank you.

Mohammed form of Muhammad.

Monroe (Irish Gaelic) from the mouth of the Roe River. *Monro, Munro, Munroe*

Montague (French) from the pointed mountain. *Monte, Monty*

Monte (Latin) mountain. Short form of Montague. *Montgomery.*

Montgomery (Old English) from the rich man's mountain. *Monte, Monty*

Moore (Old French) dark-skinned.

Mordecai (Hebrew) warrior. *Mort, Mortie, Morty*

Morey common form of Maurice; Morris; Morse; Seymour. *Morie, Morrie, Morry*

Morgan (Scottish Gaelic) from the edge of the sea.

Morley (Old English) from the meadow on the moor. *Morlee, Morly*

Morris (English) form of Maurice. *Morey, Morie, Morrie, Morry*

Morse (Old English) son of Maurice. *Morey, Morrie, Morry*

Mort short form of Mordecai; Mortimer. *Mortie, Morty*

Mortimer (Old French) still water. *Mort, Mortie, Morty*

Morton (Old English) from the town near the moor.

Moses (Hebrew) saved. *Moe, Moise, Moshe, Moss*

Mtumwa (African) pledged.

Mugaba (African) given by God.

Muhammad (Arabic) praised one. *Amed, Ahmad, Hamid, Hammad, Mahmet, Mahmoud, Mohammed*

Mukisa (African) good luck.

Murdock (Scottish Gaelic) wealthy sailor. *Murdoch*

Murray (Scottish Gaelic) sailor.

Mustafa (Arabic) superior; royal.

Muwanga (African) the Creator.

Myron (Greek) fragrant essence. *Ron, Ronnie, Ronny*

N

Naaman (Hebrew) pleasant.

Nabil (Arabic) noble.

Nachman (Hebrew) comforter.

Nadim (Arabic) friend.

Naftali (Hebrew) wreath.

Nahele (American Indian) grove of trees.

Naji (Arabic) of noble descent.

Nakisisa (African) child of the shadows.

Nam (Vietnamese) scrape off.

Namaka (Hawaiian) the eyes.

Namid (American Indian) the star dancer.

Nangwaya (African) do not trifle with me.

Nanyamka (African) God's gift.

Naoko (Japanese) straight; honest.

Narain (Hindu) name for god, Vishnu, protector of the world.

Narkis (Basque/Greek) daffodil.

Narve (Dutch) healthy and strong.

Nasim (Arabic) fresh air; (Perisan) fresh air.

Nat, Nate short forms of Nathan; Nathaniel.

Nathan (Hebrew) gift. Short form of Nathaniel. *Nat, Nate*

Nathaniel (Hebrew) gift of God. *Nat, Nate, Nathan, Natty*

Nayati (American Indian) the wrestler.

Neal (Irish) form of Neil.
Nealy

Ned common form of
names beginning with Ed.
Neddie, Neddy

Nehemiah (Hebrew)
compassion of Jehovah.
Nechemya

Neil (Irish Gaelic)
champion. *Neal, Neale,
Neils, Niel, Niels, Niles,
Nils*

Nels (Scandinavian) form
of Neil; Nelson.

Nelson (English) son of
Neil. *Neils, Niles, Nils,
Nilson*

Nestor (Greek) traveler;
wisdom.

Neville (Old French)
from the new town. *Nev,
Nevil, Nevile*

Nevin (Irish Gaelic)
worshipper of the saint;
(Old English) nephew.

Ngozi (African) blessing.

Ngu (Vietnamese) sleep.

Nicodemus (Greek)
conqueror of the people.
Nick, Nickey

Nicholas (Greek) victory
of the people. *Cole, Colin,
Klaus, Niccolo, Nichols,
Nick, Nickey, Nickie,
Nickolas, Nickolaus,
Nicky, Nicol, Nicolai,
Nicolas, Niki, Nikita,
Nikolaus*

Nick short form of
Nicholas. *Nickie, Nicky*

Niels (Scandinavian)
champion. Form of Neil;
Nelson. *Niles, Nils*

Nigel (Latin) black. *Nye*

Nehru (Indian) canal.

Noah (Hebrew)
wandering; rest. *Noach*

Noam (Hebrew) pleasant.

Noble (Latin) well-born.

Nodin (American Indian)
the wind. *Noton.*

Noel (French) the
Nativity; born at
Christmas.

Nohea (Hawaiian) handsome.

Nolan (Irish Gaelic) famous; noble. *Noland*

Norbert (Scandinavian) brilliant hero. *Bert, Bertie, Berty, Norbie, Norby*

Norman (Old French) Norseman. *Norm, Normand, Normie, Normy*

Norris (Old French) man from the north; nurse.

Northrop (Old English) from the north farm. *North, Northrup*

Norton (Old English) from the northern town.

Nosakhere (African) God's way is the only way.

Nuncio (Latin) messenger. *Nunzio*

Nuri (Arabic) shining; (Hebrew) fire.

Nuru (African) born in daylight.

Nuwamanya (African) omniscient.

Nye (Middle English) islander. Common form of Nigel.

O

Oakley (Old English) oak tree field. *Oakes*

Oba (African) king.

Obadiah (Hebrew) servant of God. *Obadias, Obediah, Obie, Oby*

Octavio (Latin) eighth. *Octavian, Octavius, Tavey.*

Oded (Hebrew) encourage.

Odell (Scandinavian) little and wealthy. *Dell, Ode, Odey, Odie, Ody*

Odokota (American Indian) friendly.

Odom (African) oak tree.

Ogden (Old English) from the oak valley or hill. *Ogdan, Ogdon*

Ogima (American Indian) chief.

Ojo (African) difficult delivery.

Olaf (Scandinavian) descendants. *Olav, Ole, Olin*

Olamina (African) this is my wealth.

Oleg (Russian) holy. *Olezka*

Olin (English) form of Olaf.

Oliver (Latin) olive tree; (Scandinavian) kind, affectionate. *Nollie, Nolly, Olivero, Olivier*

Oliwa (Hawaiian) olive tree.

Olujimi (African) God gave me this.

Omar (Arabic) first son; highest; follower of the Prophet. *Omari*

On (Chinese) peace.

Oren (Hebrew) pine tree; (Irish Gaelic) pale-complected. *Oran, Orin, Oris, Orren, Orrin*

Onkar (Indian) name of a god; indicates attributes of pure being.

Orestes (Greek) mountain man. *Oreste*

Ori (Hebrew) my light.

Orion (Greek) son of fire.

Orlando (Old English) from the famous land. *Land, Lannie, Lanny, Orland*

Orman (Old German) mariner or shipman. *Ormand*

Orneet (Hebrew) light; cedar tree.

Orrin form of Oren.

Orson (Latin) bearlike. *Sonnie, Sonny*

Orville (Old French) from the golden estate.

Osborn (Old English) warrior of God;

(Scandinavian) divine bear. *Osborne, Ozzie, Ozzy*

Oscar (Scandinavian) warrior. *Oskar, Osker, Oszkar*

Osgood (Old English) divinely good. *Ozzie, Ozzy*

Oswald (Old English) having power from God. *Oswell, Ozzie, Ozzy, Waldo*

Otis (Old English) son of Otto; (Greek) keen of hearing.

Otto (Old German) rich, prosperous.

Ouray (American Indian) the arrow.

Oved (Hebrew) worshipper; worker.

Owodunni (African) it is nice to have money.

Owen (Welsh) well-born. Form of Eugene; Evan. *Ewen*

Oxford (Old English) from the river crossing of the oxen.

𝒫

Paco (Italian) to pack; (American Indian) bald eagle.

Paddy (Irish) common form of Patrick

Pakelika (Hawaiian) noble. Form of Patrick.

Palani (Hawaiian) free man.

Palmer (Old English) palm bearing pilgrim.

Parker (Middle English) guardian of the park.

Parnell (Old French) little Peter. *Nellie, Nelly, Pernell*

Park (Chinese) the cypress tree.

Pascal (Italian) pertaining to Easter or Passover; born at Easter or Passover. *Pascale, Pace, Pasquale*

Pat short form of names containing Pat. *Pattie, Patty*

Patrick (Latin) nobleman. *Paddie, Paddy, Pat, Patsy*

Patton (Old English) from the warrior's estate.

Paul (Latin) small. *Pablo, Paolo*

Pavit (Indian) pious; pure.

Payat (American Indian) he is coming.

Pedro (Spanish) form of Peter.

Penn (Old English) enclosure; (Old German) commander. Short form of Penrod.

Penrod (Old German) famous commander. *Pen, Penn, Roddy*

Pepin (Old German) petitioner. *Pepi, Peppi, Peppie, Peppy*

Percival (Old French) pierce-the-valley. *Parsifal, Perceval, Percy, Purcell*

Percy (French) from Percy. Short form of Percival.

Perry (Middle English) pear tree; (Old French) little Peter. Common form of Peter. *Parry*

Peta (American Indian) golden eagle.

Peter (Greek) rock. *Pedro, Perry, Pete, Petey, Pierce, Pierre, Pietro, Piotr*

Petro (Russian) stone. *Petruno, Petruso*

Peyton (Old English) from the warrior's estate. *Pate, Payton*

Phil short form of Filbert; Filmore; Philip.

Phillip (Greek) lover of horses. *Felipe, Filippo, Phil, Philipp, Phillipe*

Phineas (Hebrew) oracle.

Phuoc (Vietnamese) good.

Pierre (French) form of Peter.

Pili (African) the second born.

Pinchos (Hebrew) dark-complected. *Pinye*

Plato (Greek) broad-shouldered.

Prescott (Old English) from the priest's cottage. *Scott, Scottie, Scotty*

Primo (Italian) first; firstborn.

Purdy (Indian) recluse.

Purvis (English/French) to provide food.

Putnam (Old English) dweller by the pond.

Q

Qabil (Arabic) able.

Qabiyl (Arabic) possession. *Cain*

Qasim (Arabic) divider.

Quaashie (African) born on Sunday.

Quanah (American Indian) fragrant.

Quentin (Latin) fifth; fifth-born child. *Quinn, Quint, Quintin*

Qimat (Indian) value; price.

Quinby (Scandinavian) from the queen's estate.

Quincy (Old French) from the fifth son's estate. *Quentin.*

Quinlan (Irish Gaelic) physically strong. *Quinn*

Quinn (Irish Gaelic) wise. Short form of Quentin; Quincy; Quinlan.

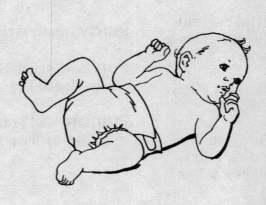

R

Rabi (Arabic) breeze; spring.

Rafael (Spanish) form of Raphael. *Rafe, Raffaello*

Rafe (Teutonic) house wolf. Short form of Rafferty; Ralph; Raphael. *Ralph, Randolph, Randal*

Rafferty (Irish Gaelic) rich and prosperous. *Rafe, Raff*

Rafi (Arabic) exalting.

Rafiq (Arabic) kind; friend.

Raiden (Japanese) thunder god.

Raini (American Indian) a god who created the world.

Raleigh (Old English) from the deer meadow. *Lee, Leigh*

Ralph (Old English) wolf counselor. *Rafe, Raoul, Rolf*

Ramon (Spanish) form of Raymond.

Ramsay (Old English) from the ram's island; from the raven's island. *Ram, Ramsey*

Rand (Old English) shield; warrior. Short form of Randall; Randolph.

Randall modern form of Randolph. *Rand, Randal, Randell, Randy*

Randolph (Old English) wolf painted on a shield; shield-wolf. *Randall, Randolf, Randy*

Randy short form of Randall; Randolph. *Randi, Randie*

Ranit (Hebrew) song. *Ronit*

Raoul (French) form of Ralph; Rudolph. *Raul*

Raphael (Hebrew) God heals. *Rafael, Rafaello, Rafe, Ray*

Rashid (Arabic) rightly guided; having true faith. *Rashidi*

Ravi (Hindi) sun. *Ravid, Raviv*

Ravid (Hebrew) wander. *Arvad, Arvid*

Ray (Old French) kingly; king's title. Short form of names beginning with the sound Ray.

Rayburn (Old English) from the deer brook. *Ray*

Raymond (Old English) mighty or wise protector. *Ramon, Ray*

Raynor (Scandinavian) mighty army.

Redford (Old English) from the red river crossing. *Ford, Red, Redd*

Redmond (Old German) protecting counselor. *Redmund*

Reece (Welsh) enthusiastic. *Reese, Rhys, Rice*

Reed (Old English) red-haired. *Read, Reade, Reid*

Regan (Irish Gaelic) little king. *Reagan, Reagen, Regen*

Reginald (Old English) powerful and mighty. *Reg, Reggie, Reggis, Reinaldo, Reinhold, Rene, Reynold, Reynolds, Rinaldo*

Remington (Old English) from the raven estate. *Rem, Tony*

Remus (Latin) fast moving.

Renato (Latin) reborn.

Rene (French) reborn. Short form of Reginald.

Reuben (Hebrew) behold, a son. *Reuven, Ruben, Rubin, Ruby*

Rex (Latin) king.

Reynold (English) form of Reginald. *Renado, Renaldo, Renato, Reynolds*

Rhett (Welsh) form of Reece.

Rich short form of Richard. *Richie, Richy, Ritchie*

Richard (Old German) powerful ruler. *Dick, Ricardo, Rich, Richie, Rick, Rickey, Rickie, Ricky, Rico, Ritchie*

Richmond (Old German) powerful protector.

Rick short form of Richard; names containing the sound Rick. *Ric, Rickie, Ricky, Rik*

Rider (Old English) horseman. *Ryder*

Riley (Irish Gaelic) valiant. *Reilly*

Rip (Dutch) ripe, fullgrown. Short form of Ripley. Common form of Robert.

Ripley (Old English) from the shouter's meadow. *Lee, Leigh, Rip*

Roarke (Irish Gaelic) famous ruler. *Rorke, Rourke*

Rob short form of Robert.

Robert (Old English) bright fame. *Bob, Bobby, Rip, Rob, Robbie, Roberto, Robin, Rupert*

Robin common form of Robert. Short form of Robinson.

Robinson (English) son of Robert. *Robin, Robinet*

Rochester (Old English) from the stone camp. *Chester, Chet, Rock, Rockie, Rocky*

Rock (Old English) from the rock. Short form of Rochester. *Rocky*

Rockwell (Old English) from the rocky spring.

Rocky modern form of Rochester.

Rod short form of names beginning with Rod. *Rodd, Roddie, Roddy*

Roderick (Old German) famous ruler. *Rod, Roddy, Roderic, Rodrick, Rodrigo, Rory*

Rodger form of Roger.

Rodney (Old English) from the island clearing. *Rod, Rodd, Roddie, Roddy*

Roger (Old German) famous spearman. *Rodger, Rog, Rogerio, Rogers, Ruggiero, Rutger*

Roland (Old German) from the famous land. *Lannie, Rolando, Rollie, Rollins, Rollo, Rowland*

Rolf (Old German) famous wolf; (German) form of Ralph. Short form of Rudolph. *Rolfe, Rollo, Rolph*

Roman (Latin) from Rome.

Romeo (Italian) pilgrim to Rome.

Romulus (Latin) citizen of Rome.

Ron short form of Aaron; Ronald. *Ronnie, Ronny*

Ronald (Scottish) form of Reginald. *Ron, Ronnie, Ronny*

Rooney (Irish Gaelic) red-haired. *Rowan, Rowen*

Roosevelt (Old Dutch) from the rose field.

Rory (Irish Gaelic) red king; (Irish) common form of Roderick.

Roscoe (Scandinavian) from the deer forest. *Rosco, Ross*

Ross (Old French) red; (Scottish Gaelic) headland. Short form of Roscoe.

Roswald (Old English) from a field of roses. *Ross, Roswell*

Roth (Old German) red hair.

Roy (Old French) king. Short form of Royal; Royce.

Royce (Old English) son of the king. *Roy*

Rudolph (Old German) famous wolf. *Raoul, Rolf, Rolfe, Rollo, Rudolf, Rudolfo, Rudy*

Rudy short form of names beginning with Rud.

Rudyard (Old English) from the red enclosure. *Ruddie, Rudy*

Rufus (Latin) red-haired. *Rufe*

Ruggiero (Teutonic) famous warrior. *Ruggero, Rogero*

Rupert (Italian/Spanish) form of Robert.

Russ short form of Cyrus; Ruskin; Russell.

Russell (French) red-haired; fox-colored. *Russ, Rustie, Rusty*

Rusty (French) redhead. Short form of Russell.

Ryan (Irish Gaelic) little king. *Ryun*

S

Saadya (Hebrew) God's helper.

Sa'id (Arabic) happy. *Saeed*

Sakima (American Indian) king.

Salim (Arabic) peace; safe. *Saleem, Salem*

Salvatore (Italian) savior. *Sal, Sallie, Salvador*

Sam (Hebrew) to hear. Short form of Samson; Samuel. *Sammie, Sammy, Shem*

Samir (Arabic) entertaining companion (male).

Samson (Hebrew) like the sun. *Sam, Sammie, Sammy, Sampson, Shem*

Samuel (Hebrew) heard or asked of God. *Sam, Sammie, Sammy, Samuele, Shem, Shmuel*

Samuru (Japanese) his name is God.

Sanborn (Old English) from the sandy brook. *Sandy*

Sancho (Latin) sanctified.

Sanders (Middle English) son of Alexander. *Sander, Sanderson, Sandor, Sandy*

Sandy common form of Alexander. Short form of names beginning with San.

Sanford (Old English) from the sandy river crossing. *Sandy*

Sang-Ook (Korean) always well.

Sargent (Old French) army officer. *Sarge, Sergeant, Sergent*

Saul (Hebrew) asked for. *Sol, Sollie, Solly*

Sawyer (Middle English) sawer of wood. *Saw, Sawyere*

Saxon (Old English) swordsman. *Sax*

Schuyler (Dutch) sheltering. *Sky, Skye, Skyler*

Scott (Old English) Scotsman. *Scot, Scotti, Scottie, Scotty*

Seamus (Irish) form of James. *Shamus*

Sean (Irish) form of John. *Shane, Shaughn, Shaun, Shawn*

Sebastian (Latin) venerated; majestic. *Sebastiano*

Selby (Old English) from the village by the mansion.

Seldon (Old English) from the willow tree valley. *Don, Donnie, Donny, Shelden*

Selig (Old German) blessed. *Zelig*

Selwyn (Old English) friend from the palace. *Selwin, Winnie, Wyn, Wynn*

Serge (Latin) attendant. *Sergei, Sergio*

Seth (Hebrew) substitute; appointed.

Seward (Old English) victorious defender.

Seymour (Old French) from St. Maur. *Maurice, Morey, Morie, Morrie*

Shakir (Arabic) thankful.

Shamus (Irish) form of James.

Shane (Irish) form of John (through Sean). *Shaine, Shayne*

Shannon (Irish Gaelic) small and wise.

Sharif (Arabic) honest.

Shawn (Irish) form of John.

Shea (Irish Gaelic) from the fairy fort. *Shae, Shay*

Shelby (Old English) from the ledge estate. *Shell, Shelley, Shelly*

Sheldon (Old English) from the farm on the ledge. *Shell, Shelley, Shelly, Shelton*

Shelomo (Hebrew) peaceable. *Shlomo, Solomon*

Shelley common form of Shelby; Sheldon. *Shell, Shelly*

Shen (Chinese) spirit; deep thought.

Shepherd (Old English) shepherd. *Shep, Shepard, Sheppard*

Sheridan (Irish Gaelic) wild man. *Dan, Danny*

Sherlock (Old English) fair-haired.

Sherman (Old English) shearer. *Mannie, Manny, Sherm, Shermie*

Sherwin (Middle English) swift runner. *Winn, Winnie, Wyn*

Sherwood (Old English) from the bright forest. *Wood, Woodie, Woody*

Shim'on (Hebrew) hearing, with acceptance. *Simeon, Simon*

Shiro (Japanese) fourth-born son.

Sid short form of Sidney.

Sidney (Old French) from St. Denis. *Sid, Sydney*

Siegfried (Old German) victorious peace..*Sig, Sigfrid, Sigfried*

Sigmund (Old German) victorious protector. *Sig, Sigismondo, Sigismund, Sigismundo*

Silas (Latin) Silvanus (the forest god). *Silvan, Silvano, Silvio, Sylvan*

Simon (Hebrew) he who hears. *Si, Sim, Simeon, Simone*

Sinclair (Old French) from St. Clair. *Clair, Clare*

Sisi (African) born on a Sunday.

Siwili (American Indian) long tail of the fox.

Skelly (Irish Gaelic) storyteller. *Skell*

Skip (Scandinavian) shipmaster. *Skipp, Skipper, Skippie, Skippy*

Slade (Old English) child of the valley.

Sloan (Irish Gaelic) warrior. *Sloane.*

Smith (Old English) blacksmith. *Smitty*

Solomon (Hebrew) peaceful. *Sol, Sollie, Solly, Zollie, Zolly*

Son (American Indian) star; (Vietnamese) mountain.

Spencer (Middle English) dispenser of provisions. *Spence, Spense, Spenser*

Stacy (Medieval) stable; prosperous. *Stace, Stacey*

Stafford (Old English) from the riverbank landing place.

Stanford (Old English) from the rocky ford. *Ford, Stan, Standford, Stanfield*

Stanislaus (Slavic) stand of glory. *Stan, Stanislas, Stanislaw*

Stanley (Old English) from the rocky meadow. *Stan*

Stanton (Old English) from the stony farm. *Stan, Stanwood*

Stephen (Greek) crown. *Esteban, Estevan, Etienne, Stefan, Stefano, Steffen, Stephan, Steve, Steven*

Sterling (Old English) valuable. *Stirling*

Sterne (Middle English) austere. *Stearn, Stearne*

Steve short form of Stephen. *Stevie, Stevy*

Steven form of Stephen.

Stewart form of Stuart. *Steward*

Stuart (Old English) caretaker; steward. *Steward, Stewart, Stu*

Suhail (Arabic) gentle; easy.

Sulaiman (Arabic) peaceful. *Solomon*

Sullivan (Irish Gaelic) black-eyed. *Sully*

Sultan (African) ruler.

Sumner (Middle English) church officer; summoner.

Sutherland (Scandinavian) from the southern land. *Sutherlan*

Sutton (Old English) from the southern town.

Sven (Scandinavian) youth. *Svend, Swen*

Sying (Chinese) star.

Sylvester (Latin) from the woods. *Silvester, Sly*

T

Tab (Middle English) drummer. *Taber, Tabor*

Tad (Polish) common form of Thaddeus.

Tadeo (Spanish, Latin) praise. *Tadeas*

Tahir (Arabic) clean, pure.

Takeshi (Japanese) unbending.

Tal (Hebrew) dew or rain. *Talor*

Talbot (Old German/French) bright valley. *Talbert, Tallie, Tally*

Talib (Arabic) seeker.

Tam (Vietnamese) the number eight.

Tamir (Arabic) one who owns date palm trees.

Tanner (Old English) leather worker; tanner. *Tan, Tanney, Tannie, Tanny*

Tano (African) river Tano.

Tate (Middle English) cheerful.

Tavish (Irish Gaelic) twin. *Tav, Tavis, Tevis*

Tayib (Indian) good or delicate.

Taylor (Middle English) tailor. *Tailor*

Ted common form of names beginning with Ed; Ted. *Tedd, Teddie, Teddy, Tedman*

Templeton (Old English) from the town of the temple. *Temp, Temple*

Terence (Latin) smooth. *Terrance, Terrence, Terry*

Terrill (Old German) belonging to Thor; martial. *Terrell, Tirrell*

Terry common form of Terence. *Terri*

Thabit (Arabic) firm.

Thaddeus (Greek) courageous; (Latin) praiser. *Tad, Taddeo, Taddeusz, Thad, Thaddaus*

Thane (Old English) attendant warrior; thane. *Thain, Thaine, Thayne*

Thanh (Vietnamese) finish.

Thatcher (Old English) roof thatcher. *Thacher, Thatch, Thaxter*

Thayer (Old French) from the nation's army.

Theo short form of names beginning with Theo.

Theobald (Old German) people's prince. *Ted, Tedd, Teddy, Theo, Thibaud, Tibold*

Theodore (Greek) gift of God. *Feodor, Teador, Ted, Teddie, Teddy, Teodor, Theo, Theodor, Théodore*

Thomas (Arabic/Hebrew) twin. *Thom, Tom, Tomas, Tomaso, Tomkin, Tommie, Tommy*

Thor (Scandinavian) thunder. *Thorin, Thorvald, Tyrus*

Thorbjorn (Scandinavian) Tor-bear.

Thorndike (Old English) from the thorny embankment. *Thorn, Thorny*

Thornton (Old English) from the thorny farm. *Thorn, Thorny*

Thorpe (Old English) from the village.

Thuc (Vietnamese) aware.

Thurston (Scandinavian) Thor's stone.

Tim short form of Timothy. *Timmie, Timmy*

Timothy (Greek) honoring God. *Tim, Timmie, Timmy*

Titus (Greek) of the giants. *Tito, Titos*

Tobias (Hebrew) the Lord is good. *Tobiah, Tobie, Tobin, Toby*

Toby common form of Tobias. *Tobie*

Todd (Middle English) fox. *Toddie, Toddy*

Tokala (American Indian) fox.

Tom short form of Thomas. *Tommie, Tommy*

Tomi (Japanese) rich.

Tony common form of Anthony; names ending in Ton. *Toni, Tonnie*

Tor (African) king.

Torrance (Irish Gaelic) from the knolls. *Torey, Torr, Torrence, Torrin, Torry*

Toshihiro (Japanese) wise.

Townsend (Old English) from the town's end. *Town, Towney, Towny*

Tracy (Irish Gaelic) battler; (Latin) courageous. *Tracey, Tracie*

Trahern (Welsh) strong as iron. *Tray*

Travis (Old French) at the crossroads. *Traver, Travers*

Tremain (Celtic) from the house of stone. *Tremaine, Tremayne*

Trent (Latin) torrent. *Trenton*

Trevor (Irish Gaelic) prudent. *Trev*

Trey (Middle English) three; the third.

Tristan (Welsh) sorrowful. *Tristam, Tristram*

Troy (Irish Gaelic) foot soldier.

Truman (Old English) faithful man.

Trygve (Scandinavian) brave victor. *Tryg*

Tucker (Old English) fuller or tucker of cloth. *Tuck, Tucky*

Tully (Irish Gaelic) he who lives with the peace of God. *Tull, Tulley*

Tung (Chinese) all, universal.

Turner (Latin) one who works the lathe.

Tuvya (Hebrew) God's goodness. *Tuvyahu, Tobiah, Tobias*

Tuyen (Vietnamese) angel.

Ty short form of names beginning with Ty.

Tyee (American Indian) chief.

Tyler (Old English) maker of tiles. *Ty, Tye*

Tynan (Irish Gaelic) dark. *Ty, Tye*

Tyrone (Greek) sovereign; (Irish Gaelic) land of Owen. *Ty, Tye*

Tyrus (English) form of Thor. *Ty, Tye*

Tyson (Old French) firebrand. *Ty, Tye*

Tzadok (Hebrew) just. *Zadok*

Tzion (Hebrew) sunny mountain. *Zion*

Tzvi (Hebrew) deer. *Zevi*

U

Ubadah (Arabic) servant of God.

Uberto (Teutonic) bright mind. *Umberto*

Udell (Old English) from the yew tree valley. *Del, Dell, Udale, Udall*

Ugo (Teutonic) intelligence; spirit.

Uilleam (Gaelic) resolute soldier. From William.

Ulf (Scandinavian) wolf.

Ulric (Old German) wolf-ruler. *Ric, Rick, Ricky, Ulrich, Ulrick*

Ulysses (Latin/Greek) Odysseus; wrathful.

Umar (Arabic) Old Arabic name. *Omar, Omer*

Upton (Old English) from the upper town.

Uriah (Hebrew) light of God. *Uri, Yuri, Yuria*

Uriel (Hebrew) God is my flame. *Uri, Yuri*

Uzumati (American Indian) grizzly bear.

Uzziel (Hebrew) God is strong; a mighty force. *Uziel, Uzziah*

$\mathcal{V}$

Valdemar (Scandinavian) famous power.

Valentine (Latin) strong; healthy. *Val, Valentin, Valentino*

Valeri (Slavic) strong; brave. *Valera, Valerik*

Valter (Scandinavian) powerful ruler. *Walter*

Van (Dutch) of noble descent. Short form of many Dutch surnames.

Vance (Middle English) thresher.

Vasilis (Greek) kingly. *Vasos, Vacileios*

Vassily (Slavic, German) royal; unwavering protector.

Vaughn (Celtic) small. *Vaughan, Von*

Velvel (Hebrew) wolf.

Vern short form of Vernon.

Vernon (Latin) spring like; youthful. *Vern, Verne*

Victor (Latin) conqueror. *Vic, Vick, Viktor, Vittorio*

Vidar (Scandinavian) tree warrior.

Vidor (Latin) conqueror.

Viho (American Indian) chief.

Vijay (Hindi) name of a god; victory.

Vilhelm (Teutonic) resolute protector.

Vincent (Latin) conquering. *Vin, Vince, Vincents, Vincenz, Vinnie, Vinny*

Vincenzo (Latin) conquerer. *Vincenzio*

Vinny common form of Vincent. *Vin, Vinnie*

Vinson (Old English) the conqueror's son. *Vin, Vinnie, Vinny*

Virgil (Latin) strong and flourishing; rod or staff bearer. *Verge, Virgilio*

Vishnu (Hindi) protector.

Vito (Latin) alive; vital. *Vite*

Vladimir (Slavic) powerful prince. *Vladamir*

Vladislav (Slavic) possesses glory. *Vladik, Vladya*

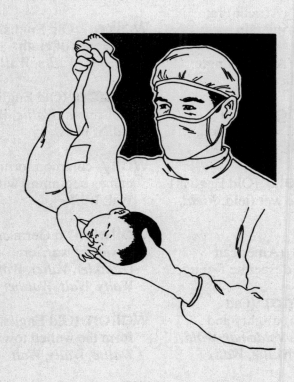

W

Waban (American Indian) the east wind.

Wade (Old English) wanderer; from the river crossing. *Wadsworth*

Wafula (African) rain; born during rain.

Wahid (Arabic) single; unequalled.

Wainwright (Old English) wagonmaker. *Wain, Wayne, Wright*

Wakefield (Old English) from the wet field. *Field, Wake*

Wakiza (American Indian) desperate fighter.

Waldemar (Old German) mighty and famous. *Valdemar, Wald, Waldo, Wallie, Wally*

Walden (Old English) from the woods. *Waldon*

Waldo (Old German) ruler. Common form of Oswald; Waldemar. *Wald, Wallie, Wally*

Waleed (Arabic/African) newborn. *Walid*

Walker (Old English) thickener of cloth; cleaner. *Wallie, Wally*

Wallace (Old English) Welshman. *Wallie, Wallis, Wally, Walsh*

Wally common form of names beginning with Wal. *Wallie*

Walter (Old German) powerful warrior. *Gauthier, Valter, Wallie, Wally, Walt, Walther*

Walton (Old English) from the walled town. *Wallie, Wally, Walt*

Wang (Chinese) hope, wish.

Wapi (American Indian) lucky.

Ward (Old English) guard. *Warden, Worden*

Warner (Old German) armed defender. *Werner, Wernher*

Warren (Old German) preserve; protector.

Washington (Old English) from a residence name. *Wash*

Wayland (Old English) from the land by the road. *Waylan, Waylon*

Wayne (Old English) wagoner. Short form of Wainwright.

Webb (Old English) weaver. *Weber, Webster*

Wells (Old English) from the springs.

Wendell (Old German) wanderer. *Wendall, Wendel*

Werner (German) form of Warner. *Wernher*

Wemusa (African) never satisfied with his possessions.

Wes short form of names beginning with Wes.

Wesley (Old English) from the western meadow. *Lee, Leigh, Wes, Westleigh, Westley*

Westbrook (Old English) from the western brook. *Brook, Brooke, Wes, West, Westbrooke*

Weston (Old English) from the western estate. *Wes, West*

Whitman (Old English) white-haired man. *Whit*

Whitney (Old English) from the white island; from fair water. *Whit*

Whittaker (Old English) from the white field. *Whit, Whitaker*

Whitby (Scandinavian) from the white dwellings.

Wilbur (German) form of Gilbert. *Wilbert, Wilburt*

Wiley (Old English) from the water meadow; from Will's meadow. *Wylie*

Wilfred (Old German) resolute and peaceful. *Wilfrid, Will, Willie, Willy*

Wiliama (Hawaiian) resolute protector. From William. *Wile, Pila*

Will short form of names beginning with the sound Will. *Willie, Willy*

Willard (Old German) resolutely brave. *Will, Willie, Willy*

William (Old German) resolute soldier; determined guardian. *Bill, Billie, Billy, Guillaume, Guillermo, Wilhelm, Will, Willie, Willis, Willy*

Win short form of names containing Win; Wyn. *Winn, Winnie, Winny*

Winfield (Old English) friendly field. *Field, Win, Winn, Winnie, Winny, Wyn*

Wing (Chinese) glory.

Winslow (Old English) friend's hill. *Win, Winn, Winnie, Winny, Wyn*

Winston (Old English) friendly town. *Win, Winn, Winnie, Winny*

Winthrop (Old English) wine village. *Win, Winn, Winnie, Winny, Wyn*

Wolfgang (Old German) advancing wolf. *Wolf, Wolfie, Wolfy*

Woodrow (Old English) passage in the woods. *Wood, Woodie, Woodman, Woody*

Woody common form of names containing Wood. *Wood, Woodie*

Worth (Old English) farmstead. *Worthington, Worthy*

Wright (Old English) carpenter. Short form of Wainwright.

Wyatt (Old French) little warrior. *Wiatt, Wye*

Wylie (Old English) charming. *Lee, Leigh, Wiley, Wye*

Wyndham (Scottish Gaelic) the village near the winding road. *Windham*

Wynn (Welsh) fair. *Winn, Winnie, Winny*

X

Xabat (Basque) from Salvatore.

Xanthe (Latin) golden-haired, yellow. *Xanthus*

Xavier (Arabic) bright; brilliant. *Javier*

Xenia (Greek) hospitable one.

Xenophon (Greek) strange voice. *Xeno, Zennie*

Xenos (Greek) stranger.

Xerxes (Persian) ruler.

Xylon (Greek) from the corner of the land.

Y

Yaakov (Hebrew) supplanter. From Jacob.

Yafeu (African) bold.

Yahya (African) God's gift.

Yancy (American Indian) Englishman. *Yance, Yancey, Yank, Yankee*

Yaphet (Hebrew) handsome. *Japhet*

Yardley (Old English) from the enclosed meadow. *Lee, Leigh, Yard*

Yasin (Arabic) name for Muhammad.

Yehuda (Hebrew) in praise of the Lord. *Judah, Yehudah, Yehudi*

Yohance (African) God's gift.

York (Old English) estate of the boar.

Young-Soo (Korean) keeping the prosperity.

Yu (Chinese) universe.

Yukio (Japanese) snow boy, one who gets his own way.

Yuma (American Indian) son of a chief.

Yuri common form of Uriah.

Yusuf (Arabic) name of a prophet; (African) he shall add to his powers. *Joseph.*

Yves (French) form of Ivar. *Ives*

Z

Zachariah (Hebrew) remembered by the Lord. *Zach, Zacharia, Zacharias, Zack, Zak*

Zachary (Hebrew) remembered by the Lord. *Zach, Zachariah, Zacharias, Zachery, Zack, Zak, Zakarias, Zeke*

Zafir (Arabic) victorious.

Zaid (Arabic) increase growth.

Zalman (Hebrew) peaceable.

Zane (English) form of John.

Zared (Hebrew) ambush.

Zebadiah (Hebrew) the Lord's gift. *Zeb*

Zebulon (Hebrew) dwelling place. *Zeb, Zebulen*

Zedekiah (Hebrew) God is mighty and just. *Zed*

Zeke short form of Ezekiel; Zachary.

Zelig (Hebrew) blessed. *Zelik*

Zeno (Greek) stranger. From Zeus. *Zenon*

Zonta (American Indian) trustworthy.

Zuberi (African) strong.

Mom's and Dad's Top 10 Lists

The following pages present a series of worksheets that will help you narrow down your choices for your baby's name. Most people don't decide on a final name until close to the very end of the pregnancy. There are many stories of children who have been named in the delivery room. Other choices may be made early and are more traditional or based on family traditions, cultural aspects, or just a favorite name you may have had in mind for years.

To use these worksheets, start by filling in your favorite girls' and boys' names. After you've had a chance to think about them, try to rank them in the order of your preferences. Then, compare them with your spouse or mate. You will probably both be surprised at the choices—there may be more similiarities than you think!

Mom's Top 10 Girls' Names

Fill in your favorite names and compare them
with Dad's list!

Mom's Rank	Name	Dad's Rank
_____	_____	_____
_____	_____	_____
_____	_____	_____
_____	_____	_____
_____	_____	_____
_____	_____	_____
_____	_____	_____
_____	_____	_____
_____	_____	_____
_____	_____	_____

Mom's Top 10 Boys' Names

Fill in your favorite names and compare them
with Dad's list!

Mom's Rank	Name	Dad's Rank
_____	_____	_____
_____	_____	_____
_____	_____	_____
_____	_____	_____
_____	_____	_____
_____	_____	_____
_____	_____	_____
_____	_____	_____
_____	_____	_____
_____	_____	_____

Dad's Top 10 Girls' Names

Fill in your favorite names and compare them
with Mom's list!

Dad's Rank	Name	Mom's Rank
_____	_____	_____
_____	_____	_____
_____	_____	_____
_____	_____	_____
_____	_____	_____
_____	_____	_____
_____	_____	_____
_____	_____	_____
_____	_____	_____
_____	_____	_____

Dad's Top 10 Boys' Names

Fill in your favorite names and compare them
with Mom's list!

Dad's Rank	Name	Mom's Rank
_____	_____	_____
_____	_____	_____
_____	_____	_____
_____	_____	_____
_____	_____	_____
_____	_____	_____
_____	_____	_____
_____	_____	_____
_____	_____	_____
_____	_____	_____

Your Family Trees

Use these next pages to list the names of your other children, your relatives, and friends, and anyone else you may think of whose names you might want to *consider* or *avoid*. Then use the next pages to fill in the names on your family trees. This will give you a good idea of the derivation of names in your own family and help you narrow down your choices.

_____   _____

_____   _____

_____   _____

_____   _____

_____   _____

_____   _____

_____   _____

_____   _____

_____   _____

_____   _____

Mom's Family

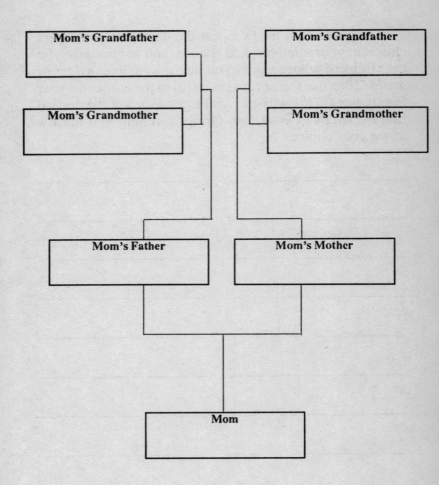

Dad's Family

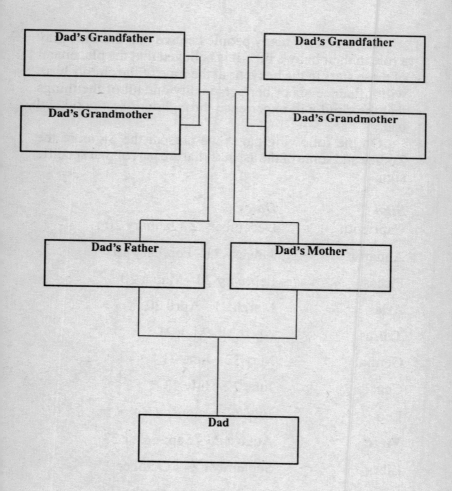

Signs of the Zodiac

As you know, many people believe that the stars play a role in their baby's life. It is believed that the placement of these stars in the heavens at the time of the child's birth will influence his or her personality and all of the things that the child will experience throughout life—good and bad.

On the following pages we present the Signs of the Zodiac and some of the aspects that are part of that specific sign.

Sign	*Dates*
Capricorn	December 22 - January 20
Aquarius	January 21 - February 19
Pisces	February 20 - March 20
Aries	March 21 - April 20
Taurus	April 21 - May 21
Gemini	May 22 - June 21
Cancer	June 22 - July 23
Leo	July 24 - August 23
Virgo	August 24 - September 23
Libra	September 24 - October 23
Scorpio	October 24 - November 22
Sagittarius	November 23 - December 21

Ruling Planets and Symbols of the Zodiac

Sign	Ruling Planet	Symbol
Capricorn	Saturn	Goat
Aquarius	Uranus	Water Bearer/Sage
Pisces	Neptune	Fish
Aries	Mars	Ram
Taurus	Venus	Bull
Gemini	Mercury	Twins
Cancer	Moon	Crab
Leo	Sun	Lion
Virgo	Mercury	Virgin
Libra	Venus	The Balances
Scorpio	Mars	Scorpion
Sagittarius	Jupiter	Archer

Elements and Stones of the Zodiac

Sign	Element	Stone
Capricorn	Earth	Garnet
Aquarius	Air	Amethyst
Pisces	Water	Bloodstone
Aries	Fire	Diamond
Taurus	Earth	Emerald
Gemini	Air	Pearl
Cancer	Water	Ruby
Leo	Fire	Sardonyx
Virgo	Earth	Sapphire
Libra	Air	Opal
Scorpio	Water	Topaz
Sagittarius	Fire	Turquoise

Flowers and Colors
of the Zodiac

Sign	Flower	Color
Capricorn	Carnation	Deep Blue
Aquarius	Violet	Light Blue
Pisces	Daffodil	Dark Purple
Aries	Daisy	Deep Red
Taurus	Lily-of-the Valley	Deep Yellow
Gemini	Rose	Violet
Cancer	Water Lily	Light Green
Leo	Gladiolus	Light Orange
Virgo	Aster	Dark Violet
Libra	Cosmos	Yellow
Scorpio	Mum	Red
Sagittarius	Narcissus	Light Purple

Bibliography

A book like this cannot be compiled without endless research. A good portion of the material came from public sources such as Ethnic Organizations as well as various government sources. There is also a wealth of information available from various state bureaus of Vital Statistics, Departments of Public Health, Bureau of Records, and other sources.

In addition to these public and organization sources, the following books were used to confirm origins and definitions of names. Often there were conflicts between the sources and we had to use several other books as tie-breakers. Where it made sense, we included multiple definitions.

Ames, Winthrop, editor, *What Shall We Name the Baby*, NY, Pocket Books, 1974.

Asante, Molefi Kete, *The Book of African Names*, NJ, Africa World Press, 1991.

Collins Gem First Names, London, William Collins Sons & Co., Ltd., 1988.

Ellefson, Connie Lockhart, *The Melting Pot Book of Baby Names*, OH, Better Way Books, 1990.

Evans, Cleveland K., Ph.D., *Unusual and Most Popular Baby Names*, NY, Signet, 1994.

Faulkner, Benjamin, *What to Name Your African Baby*, NY, St. Martin's Press, 1994.

Fields, Maxine, *Baby Names from Around the World*, Pocket Books, 1985.

Lansky, Bruce, *The Best Baby Name Book in the Whole Wide World*, NY, Meadowbrook, 1984.

Rosenkrantz, Linda, *The Last Word on First Names*, NY, St. Martin's Press, 1995.

Rule, Lareina, *Name Your Baby*, NY, Bantam Books, 1986.

Schwegel, Janet, *The Baby Name Countdown*, NY, Paragon House, 1990.

Sidi, Smadur Shir, *The Complete Book of Hebrew Baby Names*, CA, Harper San Francisco, 1989.

6,000 Names for Your Baby, NY, Dell Publishing, 1983.

The Classic 1,000 Baby Names, London, Foulsham, 1993.

Wallace, Carol McD., *20,001 Names for Baby*, NY, Avon Books, 1995.

Wilen, Joan & Lydia, *Name Me, I'm Yours*, NY, Fawcett Columbine, 1982.